ANIMALS

*Personal Tales of Encounters
with Spirit Animals*

Enjoy these other books in the Common Sentience series:

ANCESTORS: *Divine Remembrances of Lineage, Relations and Sacred Sites*

ANGELS: *Personal Encounters with Divine Beings of Light*

GUIDES: *Mystical Connections to Soul Guides and Divine Teachers*

MEDITATION: *Intimate Experiences with the Divine through Contemplative Practices*

NATURE: *Divine Experiences with Trees, Plants, Stones and Landscapes*

Learn more at sacredstories.com.

ANIMALS

*Personal Tales of Encounters
with Spirit Animals*

Mary — enjoy the critter magic!
— Gina
p. 117

Featuring

DR. STEVEN FARMER

SACRED STORIES
PUBLISHING

Books may be purchased through booksellers or by contacting Sacred Stories Publishing.

Editor: Gina Mazza

Animals: Personal Tales of Encounters with Spirit Animals
Dr. Steven Farmer

Tradepaper ISBN: 978-1-945026-86-7
EBook ISBN: 978-1-945026-87-4
Library of Congress Control Number: 2021949257

Published by Sacred Stories Publishing, Fort Lauderdale, FL USA

CONTENTS

PART ONE: UNDERSTANDING SPIRIT ANIMALS

PART TWO: PERSONAL TALES OF ENCOUNTERS WITH SPIRIT ANIMALS

PART THREE: DEEPENING YOUR CONNECTION WITH SPIRIT ANIMALS

APPENDIX: SPIRIT ANIMALS FOR SPECIFIC PURPOSES

MEET OUR SACRED STORYTELLERS

MEET OUR FEATURED AUTHOR

PART ONE

Understanding Spirit Animals

When I look into the eyes of an animal, I do not see an animal.
I see a living being. I see a friend. I feel a soul.

—ANTHONY DOUGLAS WILLIAMS

OUR INTIMATE CONNECTION
TO THE ANIMAL KINGDOM

*a*nimals of countless shapes, colors, sizes, and species are in plain sight all around us, yet have we forgotten something essential? Have we forgotten that we *are* one, as well—the human animal?

We only need to pause for a moment and feel our hearts beating, observe our movements, and consider that we eat, sleep, eliminate, and procreate in the same basic manner as nearly all other animal beings. Like them, we eventually pass from this physical world, with our bodily substances reassimilating into the soil and our timeless souls returning home to the spirit world.

In other words, animals are us; and we are them. For our long-ago ancestors and many indigenous peoples, it's a given that homo sapiens are fundamentally related to every living being on this planet—from the smallest pebble and multitude of plants to the largest mammals. In our modern world, too many of us have forgotten this intimate relationship. We may agree with it as a philosophy, but the experience of it as our true reality has been obscured, even as we breathe the same air, share the same land and oceans, and cohabitate on this single spectacular Mother Earth.

In my humble opinion, it is the animals who are faithfully and lovingly working on our behalf—both in the visible and unseen worlds—to help us reawaken to who we really are and stay on course with our evolution as a humanity. We, in turn, can give deserving reverence to the animals for doing so, and as an honoring to them, stay open to the wisdom of these Animal People, as many Native Americans call them. They have much to teach us, and that is why the personal tales being shared in this book are so much more than mystical animal encounters; they are stories illustrating how our animal brethren impart their perennial lessons to us—and, as a result, we, too, can soar like eagles, run like pumas, and reach new heights like the tallest giraffe.

In my work, I see every day that more and more individuals are returning to this truth and are curious to discover how to tune into and receive guidance from the animal world. This gives me hope for humanity!

It's actually quite wondrous how animals permeate our consciousness, and are omnipresent in our everyday lives. They surround us in physical form, like the geese that fly overhead, the rabbit that scampers across your lawn at dusk, or the dolphins that frolic just outside the ocean's surf when you're at the beach. Our animal friends appear everywhere in symbolic form, as well. I only have to look as far as my computer to see the tiny raccoon, tortoise, owl, and hawk totems sitting on a shelf behind it. The rainbow serpent in the painting behind my desk is observing me right now, and in the corner of the room, the bronze rendition of a raven with his wings spread is intently watching me. Okay, I'm known as the animal spirit guy, but glance around *your* living or work space right now. Do you see animal influences in your environment?

Our intimate connection to the animal kingdom reveals itself in a variety of ways. Even in congested urban settings, birds sing away in the trees, pigeons gather around the man on the park bench feeding them, and squirrels scamper about doing squirrel business. Taking a walk in an urban park or a rural forest, we might catch a glimpse of groundhogs rumbling through the bush, deer quietly darting away, or wild turkeys scratching for grubs. Whether we notice them or not, animals co-exist with us—sometimes to our dismay, like finding a mouse in the kitchen pantry . . . but what if that rodent, wasp, or opossum is appearing to us for a deeper reason?

Most of us have felt the desire to bring a domesticated animal into our lives as a friend and companion. It's no wonder that the pet industry is valued in the tens of billions of dollars—yes, billions. Our dogs, cats, goldfish, hamsters, and other pets compel us to remember that animals are part of our earthly "family." And we're captivated by the ones that remain feral. Wild animal parks aren't just fun places to have an outing for the day; they offer us a safe yet thrilling glimpse of the wildness that abounds in nature.

We even have the natural instinct to revere animals by naming our sports teams after them, such as the Philadelphia Eagles and Sydney Roosters, as well as various organizations like the Lion's Club or the Loyal Order of Moose. In both indigenous and contemporary cultures, individuals may be given an animal name, such as Fawn, Robin, Little Bear, Buck, Colt, or Black Tail Swan.

Popular movies, books, plays, and more integrate animals into the story line as important characters. In particular, our enduring mythological and fairy tales portray animals that communicate with each other and with humans. We keep animals close to us by wearing images of them—or their attributes, like leopard print—on our clothing and jewelry, and by incorporating them into our living space décor. Our vehicles are named after cougar and jaguar, and our puma shoes help us run faster.

Even in our everyday language, animal metaphors abound. The stock market is either a bull or a bear market; someone is busy as a beaver, or tries to weasel their way out of things. You may be trying to outfox someone, but because your idea sounds fishy, they probably think you're just horsing around and trying to get their goat. So, once they find you out, you'll have to eat crow.

You get the picture. We're so intertwined with our animal kin that most of the time, we may take for granted their ubiquity in our lives and the bountiful gifts they give us. Yet we're in a time right now when understanding the interrelationship of all sentient beings is more important to our collective survival than ever; and having a solid connection to the Life Force that animates us all is crucial. The animals can help us trust our own spiritual authority.

So, come fly with me into the magic and mystery of spirit animals!

WHAT ARE SPIRIT ANIMALS?

*T*he spirit world is not some place up in the sky far removed from us. It's another dimension that exists alongside our material reality. It is present and accessible at all times, requiring only the willingness, intention, and openness to make contact with the beings that reside there—including spirit animals. Our awareness and consciousness are the vehicles that allow us to accomplish this connection.

Spirit animals are extensions of God, Great Spirit, Source, or whatever name you give to All That Is, just as we and everything else in the material world are. They are part of a broader realm, most often referred to as spirit guides, helping spirits, or guardian spirits.

These three terms are used interchangeably to mean any of the spiritual beings that help us in a life-affirming way, such as ancestors, archangels, nature spirits—or animals. They may be ordinarily non-visible or show up in visible form, and will often indicate their presence through signs and omens. We can also call on them for guidance, protection, encouragement, and inspiration.

Some spirit guides have been with us since childhood, while others appear at various periods in our life, perhaps to help us through difficult transitions. We may see them, hear them, feel them, or just know they're with us. The important thing to remember is that they want to help us experience more peaceful, harmonious, and happier lives, yet will not interfere with our free will. They are happy to serve and willingly do so whenever called upon.

ANIMAL SPIRIT GUIDES AND SPIRIT ANIMALS

How do animals fit into the spirit world? The concept of spirit animals is found in most indigenous cultures. Their relationships with animals are the result of tens of thousands of years of ancestral connection to their environments, landscapes, and eco-systems, which they regard as sacred.

The particular meanings of different animals vary broadly across world cultures, but the commonality is that civilizations have worshipped, mythologized, and revered animals as guardians, messengers, spirits, and even gods since time immemorial. From the Buddhist belief that animals are souls that reincarnate; the Hindi depiction of monkey and elephant gods like Ganesha and Hanuman; and Egyptian deities that meld human with sphinx, ibis, falcon, snake, dog, and more; to the Greeks, Druids, other Europeans and Asians who listen for wisdom from the animals, the spiritual ties between mankind and animals is evident everywhere.

A few more terms for clarification: Spirit guides or helping spirits in the form of an animal—generally called animal spirit guides or spirit animals—appear when Spirit is attempting to get our attention. A spirit animal can show up physically, such as a crow that lands outside your window and glares at you; or symbolically, as when you see images of a sea horse everywhere you turn. They can also reveal themselves in a dream vision, or through sound, like a blue jay screeching nearby. A spirit animal can cross your path then leave as quickly as it arrived, or reveal itself repetitively over a span of time. Regardless of the duration of its presence, if it shows up in an unusual way, it's doing so as a messenger from Spirit.

I am delighted to share my perspective and personal experiences with spirit animals, as I know first-hand how profound of a supporting role they can play in helping navigate life's challenges. I have learned so much about myself through the eyes of hawk, bear, and many other spirit animal friends.

The more you enter into partnership with them, you too will experience spirit animals as exceptional teachers about the natural world, the spiritual realm, and about life overall. Working with spirit animals as part of your daily routine will not only enhance your ordinary experiences but will immensely expand your spiritual capacities, as well. Once in relationship with these animal brothers and sisters, you will come to trust their keen perception, sage advice, and the simple ways in which they appear just when you most need guidance.

TOTEM ANIMALS

Spirit animals are sometimes referred to as totem animals, although this is a more specific type of spirit animal that has a couple of different meanings. A totem animal can be one that is shared by a clan, family lineage, or like-minded group, or adopted by any type of group for a particular reason. For example, an addiction support group may decide to use a lion in symbolic form to reinforce qualities of endurance and strength of will. An intentional community might embrace the totem of a meadowlark or dove to instill qualities of relationship harmony among the members. Or a group of neighbors could choose to honor the native species in the vicinity by naming their local park Raccoon Trail or Deer Run.

Another meaning of totem animal is a favorite spirit animal that can be represented symbolically, such as with a talisman, emblem, crest, statue, or piece of jewelry. In the Pacific Northwest, totem poles have representations of the spirit animals that are shared by the various clans that exist within the tribe, often with the totem animal for the entire community being at the top of the totem pole. Even in contemporary society, you'll find representations of animals that can rightfully be called totems, such as the teddy bears or stuffed bunny rabbits we give to small children to give them comfort.

I've discovered that a more useful term for what has been called a personal totem is a *power animal,* the meaning of which stems from shamanism, as described in the following section. The ancient practice of shamanism that is seeing a revival in the contemporary world provides a different perspective on these spirit animals that work with us throughout our lifetimes. As you'll see, a power animal is a spirit animal that is much more than a symbol; it is a guardian spirit that can provide protection, guidance, and healing.

POWER ANIMALS

Spirit animals can also grace our lives in the form of power animals. This is a highly personal and specialized relationship with an animal spirit guide. It's not one you choose in the usual sense of the word; it's more of a soul-to-soul connection, in which your soul bonds with the soul—or, more accurately, the oversoul—of the animal. The power animal relationship is one to be nurtured and attended to on a regular basis, and usually lasts for a number of years.

The concept of power animal has its origins in shamanism, and the term "shaman" originates from the Tungus people of Siberia and means "one who knows." It is believed that the advent of shamans occurred after agriculture was discovered. In various indigenous cultures up to the present day, you will find shamans who are an essential part of these communities.

The fundamental skill of the shaman is the shamanic journey—that is, an altered state of awareness in which the shaman transports his soul into non-ordinary reality to align with helping spirits and receive teachings, guidance, and healings. This is done by reconnecting the conscious human life with the natural and spirit worlds through animal spirits.

For this reason, during shamanic journeys, power animals are critical allies for the shaman. In essence, the power animal aids the shaman in transcending the earthly plane and attuning to the ethereal. A shaman's particular power animal is typically acquired early in their initiation into their practice. From then on, the power animal travels with the shaman whenever he goes on a journey, for himself or on behalf of others.

These days, many more people are becoming familiar with shamanism, and some feel called to work as a shamanic practitioner. I am honored to serve in this role in my work. Whenever I do a shamanic journey, I always call on two of my four power animals: Wolf and Raven. Wolf has proven to be a supreme protector and guardian, as well as a guide; and Raven has proven to be an excellent manifester, guide, and consultant.

In these sessions, I serve as the bridge for my clients to meet their own power animals. It is always a profound and magical experience for myself and the individual, as no two journeys are alike. Sharon, for example, met her power animal in a journey and was surprised that Dolphin came to her. As we worked together in her sessions, it became evident that this was the perfect power animal for her, as Dolphin provided the powers of communication, playfulness, breathwork, and a greater fluidity in her physical movements. Sharon eventually realized that Dolphin's characteristics were subtly helping her modify habits in her life that needed greater balance and flow.

You don't need to be a shaman, have an interest in shamanism, or be associated with an indigenous culture to experience the tremendous value of working with power animals. You can learn to access this same energy by opening to the possibility of these intelligent beings guiding you. In response, the animals will answer your heart's calling. It may come to you in a meditation, vision, or dream to impart spiritual wisdom or guidance.

Power animals can stay with you for extended periods of time and for specific reasons. I've observed that they enter into our lives at a time when we most need their particular expression of spiritual power. For instance, if you're a manager or leader who is dealing with hostile team members, Crab can step in sideways to assist you in making quick decisions, turning things around, and tactfully deal with confrontation. If you're going through a major life transition like a divorce or career change, you may find Albatross flying in to help lift your burdens, or Camel replenishing your faith when you feel discouraged or lost.

Your power animal may leave you at some point, which usually means that the relationship has served its purpose, and another one is or will be coming into your life.

Because a spirit animal's power is drawn from its instinctual and wild nature, domesticated animals cannot be power animals; they've lost much of their wildness and are removed from the natural world. Likewise, some traditions believe that insects are excluded from being power animals because of their size and nature, as are mythological animals such as dragons and unicorns, which I will speak more about later. I found it fascinating that when I was writing my book on power animals, Dragonfly, Butterfly, and other insects argued vehemently about being included, so I included them. I now see the wisdom of that, as insects offer unique types of power.

THE ESSENCE OF THE SPIRIT ANIMAL

Depending on how and in what way they show up in the material world— whether in the flesh or as a symbol—the appearance of animal spirit guides can be as a representative of the consciousness of that animal. For instance, if your power animal is a crane, the traits of longevity and honor that you glean from it are coming not just from a single bird, but from the entire species of cranes.

Throughout these pages, you will notice that I am either referring to animal spirit guides as particular beings, such as badgers and chameleons, or as the essence of these beings—hence, Badger or Chameleon. The hummingbird that flits about and then hovers for several seconds directly in front of you isn't just a hummingbird but is carrying with her the essence of *all* hummingbirds, and is therefore Hummingbird with a capital "H." That's also why when speaking of animal spirits, it is appropriate to leave out the "a" or "an"; the hawk that visits you isn't only a hawk, but in some instances, also represents the consciousness of all hawks . . . and is, therefore, Hawk.

Why is this distinction important? Viewing your animal spirit guides in this expansive way will most likely inspire you to have a greater and deeper appreciation for all cranes, all badgers, all hummingbirds, and to extend that care and respect to the animal kingdom as a whole. If Shark is your power animal, for example, the love and appreciation you feel for Shark will naturally span out to encompass all creatures of the sea, then those of the land and the air. Eventually, this will translate into a desire to walk more gently on Mother Earth, and feel compassion for her as a living being.

This is why I feel strongly that co-creating our earthly existence with spiritual guidance from our animal brethren can truly change all of our lives for the better. Now let's delve into the specifics of how spirit animals fulfill this grand purpose.

WHAT IS THE PURPOSE
OF SPIRIT ANIMALS?

*S*ales reps. That's what I sometimes call animals who visit us in various ways on behalf of Great Spirit. They are intermediaries who are able to connect us to God, Source, the Creator, as a specific physical manifestation of Great Spirit.

It is my belief that Spirit does not express through us but, more accurately, that we *are* Spirit in expression, which just happens to be physicalized. I am Spirit expressing as Steven. Crow is Spirit expressing as a crow. Buffalo is Spirit expressing as a buffalo. That is why whenever animals present themselves in an unusual way or repeatedly over a short span of time, it's an indication that something very significant is going on that needs to be addressed.

SPIRIT ANIMAL SYMBOLISM

Animals express to and through us by way of symbolism. An archetypal power resides within and manifests through all creatures. These archetypes embody their own qualities and characteristics, which are reflected in the outward behaviors and activities of the animals. Snake shedding its skin, for example, becomes symbolic of letting go of things that no longer serve you. A dragonfly that reflects light on its wings and deftly changes flight patterns in midair demonstrates the ability to be flexible and welcome fresh perspectives.

Understanding the meaningful and profound wisdom of archetypal language is how you can begin to establish a personal connection to the animal that crosses your path, which can occur in the physical world, such as seeing a frog or elk, or in your meditative or dream states.

The further you immerse into the precise symbolism of the spirit animal, at some point its true essence will reveal itself to you, thereby gifting you with messages that may be universal in meaning yet feel incredibly personal. For instance, the spirit animal can symbolize aspects of your personality, feelings you may not have fully acknowledged, events or influences in your life, or skills and traits that you have successfully acquired or have yet to develop. It can represent a situation you are dealing with or emotions you are in the midst of processing. Ant, for example, may enter your life to instill qualities of discipline, industriousness, and working for the greater good. Butterfly might float into your world to show you how to lighten up, flow with the changes, and accept them as opportunities for positive growth.

While we're on the subject of archetypes, I'd like to address the concept of mythological creatures as animal spirit guides. Some people find themselves receiving messages from Dragon, Unicorn, or Phoenix, to name a few. While it can be easy to dismiss these kinds of messengers, the reality is that these non-visible beings are in our collective consciousness and, for that reason, they are "real."

In the case of these mythological animals, it is irrelevant that they are not physically embodied in the world; their teachings and wisdom are very much applicable to our lives. If a dragon comes to you through your dreams or imagination, for example, it may be suggesting that you have to put a little more fire or passion into your life. Unicorns may suggest that you need to honor your imagination more.

Whether they appear in physical or mythological form, the archetypes that spirit animals embody can aid us greatly on our path of personal and spiritual evolution.

SPIRIT ANIMALS BRING US MEDICINE

When we speak of how an animal spirit guide shows up symbolically and imparts its wisdom, we say that the animal is bringing us a certain medicine. This medicine comes in the form of wisdom, guidance, protection, power, or teachings. Each animal has specific gifts that are unique to them, so the medicine they deliver serves specific functions or purposes, such as the ones I'm giving throughout these chapters.

Pay attention to what's happening in your life when a spirit animal appears, as it's probably there to give you something that you need at that particular time. For example: Cougar = leadership. Boar = facing your fears and doing what is necessary to resolve them. Hawk = perspective, focus. The message you receive may be practical advice, or a much deeper one designed to remind you of your spiritual path and soul's journey. And as I mentioned earlier, when a power animal shows up, its medicine is one that will help support and sustain you over a longer period of time, typically many years.

I'll relay a situation that my friend, Rob, and his wife, Sue, recently shared with me. They were preparing for a major move to a new city and Rob was feeling extremely anxious about it, to the point of losing sleep and dropping weight. One night, a raccoon appeared in his back yard. He researched the meaning of Raccoon and discovered that the message was about resourcefulness.

Upon contemplation of this creature's wisdom, Rob realized that he did, in fact, have all the necessary resources, both internal and external, for this move. It relaxed him a great deal during the rest of the moving process, and he felt encouraged by Racoon's medicine to stay flexible and adapt quickly to whatever came up. The move went well, and Rob and Sue are now living very happily in their new home.

SPIRIT ANIMALS TEACH US ABOUT OURSELVES

Spirit animals clearly teach us about aspects of ourselves, including our strengths and weaknesses, our limiting beliefs, and our highest potentials. When we bond with an animal spirit guide, we are encouraged to discover and explore more aspects of ourselves.

It's quite fascinating to study the behaviors and characteristics of the animals, and relate it back to yourself. Learn all you can about the animal, including its colors, mannerisms, habitat, diet, and how it relates to others in its species. What activities does it get involved in? Is it carnivore or omnivore? Is it a pack animal or one that stands alone? Lion teaches self-confidence. Do you need to be more assertive? Squirrel is a master of activity and accumulating resources. Are you preparing for the near or distant future, or do you need to learn how to gather and ration?

Again, the more you decode the symbology and archetypal nature of the animal, the more it will teach you.

THEY ARE A BRIDGE TO THE SPIRIT WORLD

Since animals easily inhabit both the material and non-material worlds, they can serve as a conduit for delivering messages from those in spirit, including our deceased loved ones. It is fairly common for those who have lost a loved one to have an experience of a spirit animal presenting itself as—or as a reminder of—that person who has passed. For instance, a dove shows up shortly after you've lost someone close to you, lands on your table while you're outside having your coffee, and you swear it's staring right at you. You simply know that this is a messenger from your loved one saying, *I'm okay, don't worry.* A spirit animal may sometimes deliver a message that your loved one wanted to tell you when they were alive.

After my friend Miranda's father died, she went to a spot on the beach located in front of her father's favorite restaurant, and she noticed a single dolphin frolicking in the water unusually close to shore. As she walked along the beach, the dolphin followed her for several meters, then swam further out to sea and joined his pod. Miranda felt this was a very reassuring message from Dolphin that her father was just fine in the spirit world.

Animals absolutely play a role in delivering messages from Spirit by utilizing all of their attributes. Feathers, paw prints, nests, antlers, and more can show up synchronistically in the exact right place at the perfect moment . . . and in a form that you recognize as a nudge from your loved one. It is typically accompanied by a deep sense of peace.

SPIRIT ANIMALS HELP US HEAL AND EVOLVE

As you will see from the stories that others have so generously shared in this book, spirit animals can help us heal and evolve, especially those who stay with us for short or long periods of time as totem animals and power animals. They remind us in both subtle and obvious ways of how Spirit is assisting us on our life path.

I'm thinking of my client, Matt, who wanted to write but didn't feel very confident about doing so. Over a period of a couple of months, he kept running across spiders sitting in the middle of their beautiful webs. The consistent encouraging messages that came to Matt through Spider were about weaving all of his life's tales into a greater story, thereby taking solid action in writing his book.

I always enjoy sharing stories of my personal power animals, partly in honor of them, and by way of illustrating how they work in our lives. The first power animal that came to me more than 30 years ago is Snake. At the time, I had not begun my journey into shamanic realities so had no idea what spirit animals were, let alone power animals. I was attending a men's retreat when Snake came to me very strongly and quite unexpectedly during a meditation. I had no idea what it meant but it got me thinking about a physical snake's characteristics. What do they do every season? They shed, which is one of their medicines and metaphorically can reflect the natural transformational process that a person is going through. Upon pondering this, I realized that my participation in that event was helping me do just that: shed an old identity, which then transported me into a different way of being a man.

Since that first encounter with Snake, I've continued to experience an evolution in my understanding of Snake as a power animal. Over the years, I kept getting signs that confirmed this relationship and as I began studying and practicing shamanism, it became apparent that this was indeed my power animal. I discovered that another medicine of Snake Spirit is healing. These days, Snake's primary purpose is to assist me when I'm doing work as a healer. In honor of his medicine, I carry him with me via a tattoo on my arm.

Wolf has been my spiritual ally for a good 25 years. He came to me in an introductory course on core shamanism hosted by anthropologist and author Michael Harner, who has been instrumental in bringing shamanism into contemporary culture. Michael had us pair up and take turns doing power animal retrievals for each other, similar to how I described working with my clients earlier. Sometime after that, Owl came to me as a power animal, and my relationship with him has been significant in my work as a psychotherapist. Owl's medicine of seeing into the darkness has proven to be extremely useful in my therapy practice many times over, as I often deal with hidden shadows in my clients' personalities.

Owl stayed with me for about 12 years until Raven came along and sort of booted him out of the group. Owl still shows up every so often, but his status has shifted from power animal to animal spirit guide, so I still pay close attention when Owl does show up. Raven, though, in all his bluntness and cockiness, has since been a supreme guide who carries the medicine of magic and manifestation. He calls me out whenever I stray too far from the path of my life's mission.

The most recent addition to my tribe of spirit allies is Tortoise. He helps me to stay grounded and close to the earth, and also to discern when to move forward and stick my neck out, or when to pull back. Tortoise's wisdom is a good example of how the characteristics of the physical animal can become a metaphor for the kind of medicine a spirit animal can provide in its role as a power animal.

I can sense when my four power animals are present, and I offer prayers of thanks almost every day for their guidance and protection, and for the many ways that they have personally helped me heal and evolve. Snake, Wolf, Owl, Tortoise, and I have learned to collaborate well together after many years of being consciously connected.

As you can see, spirit animals play a foundational role in nearly every aspect of our lives. Doses of their medicine teach us about ourselves, help us face challenges and live more fully, and offer broader, wiser perspectives on our relationship with others and nature as a whole. Are you ready to connect with your animal allies? Turn the page and let's begin.

HOW SPIRIT ANIMALS
CONNECT WITH US

*T*he subtle ways in which spirit animals speak to us are as splendid and plentiful as the number of species on the planet. Yet overall, we receive messages from the spirit world in five major ways: visual, auditory, sensory, kinesthetic, and cognitive.

As you open to receiving guidance from spirit animals and your connection to the unseen world develops, you'll probably discover that one of these five pathways is the strongest and feels the most natural to you. Over time, a secondary sense may begin to come online, so to speak.

The only requirement is that you hold a clear intention to receive these messages and simply remain receptive . . . and they will come to you, often in unexpected and surprising ways.

Visual. This can occur with your actual eyes, or your inner eye. For instance, you may see a nest in an unusual place, or notice a skunk run across your front porch. Vision through your third eye, or *clairvoyance*, is when you see the spirit animal in the non-physical realm, such as a meditation vision or a vivid dream. When a spirit animal comes to you visually, note its colors, physical features, and how it moves. You may even detect emotion through its facial expressions or by looking into its eyes.

Auditory. You may hear the voice of a spirit animal in your mind—called *clairaudience*—giving you advice. Or, a sound in your environment may trigger a thought about an animal spirit guide—like the howl of a hyena in the hills, the cocking of a rooster on a TV show, or the lonesome cry of a whippoorwill in the melody of a country song. You may overhear a conversation or listen to someone talking, and intuitively know that what is being said is a message from a spirit animal. Messages coming in this way are typically short and to the point, without excess verbiage.

Sensory. You may feel the presence of the ethereal form of your animal spirit guide, and get a sense of what they're trying to communicate to you. This sense—or, *clairsentience*, sometimes called a gut feeling or sixth sense—is our intuition, something we are all born with. Trust that your inner sense is helping you decipher what your animal spirit guide is imparting to you.

Kinesthetic. Spirit animals also naturally connect with us through our other main senses of taste, touch, and smell. You may detect the scent of cow manure wafting through the air, or literally walk through a spiderweb on your outdoor deck. In meditation, you might taste the saltiness of ocean water that accompanies a vision of a whale. When working with a spirit animal, you may feel its presence in the form of wings brushing above your head. Your kinesthetic sense is also how a spirit animal's characteristics can show up for you; when encountering Swan, for example, you might feel its gracefulness, which translates to your feeling more graceful in your movements, as well.

Cognitive. Have you ever known something, but you don't know *how* you know it . . . you just do? This knowing through our thought processes in the form of inspiration or insight is called *claircognizance*. Similar to clairsentience, it is a primary pathway through which you animal spirit guides will speak to you. While observing a woodpecker, you might have the thought about how to drill down to a problem you are currently facing. A lizard may tell you through a thought pattern how to detach from your ego and shapeshift into a multidimensional being with greater capacities.

What's really magical is when all of the above senses come together to gift you with the story that the animal spirit is benevolently unfolding for you.

Let's say that a bright red-breasted robin repeatedly flies into your living room picture window for a couple of hours, as if it's trying to get your attention. You run out to the grocery store and notice in the floral department an arrangement of spring flowers with powder-blue robin eggs at the base. Seeing the simplicity of the delicate eggs fills you with an odd sense of melancholy, as your life has been extremely challenging lately. The eggs remind you of simpler times when you were a child.

Closing your eyes to meditate the next morning, your inner vision is flooded with a warm red hue, which energizes you and gives you a subtle sense of cheerfulness. Just as you leave for work, you hear the rolling trill of a robin in a tree near the driveway. Pausing for a moment, you walk over to the tree, then linger a few more minutes to observe the bird.

As a mother robin sits guardedly on her nest, protecting her offspring, a feeling comes over you that something fresh and exciting is about to be born as you enter a new season in your life. Feeling a buoyancy in your spirit that you haven't felt in a long time, a message arrives through your inner knowing. You hear: *Hope springs eternal . . .* and you know everything is going to be alright because Robin, metaphorically, has you covered in her nest, too.

You take another moment to thank Robin for her joyful insights before carrying on with your day—only now, you feel altered in the most lighthearted way.

That is the power of animal wisdom, and how spirit animals generously share their medicine with us.

ANCIENT AND INDIGENOUS ANIMAL WISDOM

*A*ll of us have a deep and often hidden unconscious ancestral memory of what it's like to have a sacred and intimate relationship with all manifestations of Spirit in the physical realm—particularly animals. Every one of us—whatever the color of your skin, your ethnicity, or your native language—has had ancestors who knew in their hearts and souls that we are intertwined with the natural world.

"It's not about living *on* the land," a friend recently reminded me, "It's about living *with* the land, and the subtle implications of this relationship."

Throughout the world, cultural stories of and experiences with animals and spirit animals are abundant and resonate with our instinctual connection to the animal kingdom. They convey an innate kindship with the vast number of animal beings with whom we share this planet.

As for animal spirit guides, the awareness that Spirit sometimes shows up in animal form has been inherent in the cultural beliefs of indigenous peoples for millennia. There are many variations on this theme depending on the mythos of the particular culture, but the common thread is the unquestionable acceptance of animals as spirit guides.

Totems have been used in shamanistic practice throughout human history. Hunters and warriors from ancient civilizations would scratch images of their prey on cave walls. They would perform ceremonies to bless and ensure a plentiful hunt and to acknowledge and thank the spirit of the animal being sacrificed. Ancient tribes, religions, and spiritual traditions have all in some form embedded animal symbolism into their practices.

Even various creation myths credit spirit animals as the Creator of the world, or parts of it. The Aboriginal peoples of Australia, for instance, believe that the Rainbow Serpent is the Creator of the land, and the indigenous peoples of the Pacific Northwest say that Raven was responsible for the birth of the sun, rivers, and tides.

FAMILIARS AND 'AUMAKUA

The idea of *familiars* dates back to the Middle Ages in western Europe. Familiars were mainly associated with witches, while these days, they're associated with Wiccans. Familiars are spirit guides that typically show up as animals, although they can also inhabit objects, such as rings or lockets. The familiar can also be the companion of magicians and sorcerers. Think Harry Potter's owl.

Another term for familiars that has been grossly distorted over the centuries is *daemon* or *demon*. Up until the persecution of witches that began in the late 13th century, this word did not infer something evil. The word demon got . . . well, demonized. In more contemporary terms, a demon is simply an animal spirit guide, often embodied in a companion animal, such as a cat or dog.

From ancient Hawai'ian spirituality, which is still practiced today, comes the concept of 'aumakua (ow-ma-koo-ah). 'Aumakua are the spirits of deceased ancestors. The very first 'aumakua were the children of humans who had mated with the Akua, or primary gods; the main ones are Ku (Koo), Kane (Kah-nay), Lono, and Kanaloa (Kah-nah-low-ah). When someone dies, they go through a period of time when they stay with these Akua and thereby acquire a degree of mana, or power. Eventually they can make themselves known to their descendants. One of the most prevalent ways in which they appear—although not limited to this—is through animals and animal spirits. They can also show up in the wind, rain, or lightning, or in dreams.

So, an animal spirit guide by any other name—whether called 'aumakua, a familiar, a power animal, or a totem animal—is still an animal spirit guide, the umbrella term used for these wise beings.

BECOMING UNCIVILIZED

The healer and elder Malidoma Patrice Somé, from the Dagara peoples in the small West African nation of Burkina Faso, describes how his people believe that there are three levels of intelligence on Earth. Plants are considered to be the most intelligent beings, and animals second, with humans capturing the ribbon for third place. It's a different way of looking at life and our relationship with plants and animals, one that contradicts the more typical and subtle arrogance ingrained within many of us in more civilized societies.

Whether we agree or not that we're somehow less intelligent than plants or animals, most indigenous peoples, who are more intimately connected to the natural world, know that we are intrinsically related to all life on this fair planet. Chief Seattle of the Suqwamish and Duwamish tribes of British Columbia said it best: "Humankind has not woven the web of life. We are but one thread within it. Whatever we do to the web, we do to ourselves. All things are bound together. All things connect."

So how is it that those of us who have been raised in the more civilized parts of the world have forgotten this connection? How did we forget how to talk with the animals, listen to their language, connect with their spirit, and show them compassion and gratitude for all they give us? How did we come to live in this illusion that we're somehow separate from all other beings and nature herself?

Of course, there's no single cause for this dissociation from the natural world and specifically from animals, yet we can point to a couple of powerful influences. One of these was the beginning of the scientific revolution, heralded by Sir Francis Bacon in the early 16th century. Considered the founder of modern science, Bacon claimed that goal seeking was a specifically human activity, and attributing goals to nature misrepresents it as humanlike.

It became science's job to objectify nature, and critical thinking otherwise became a cardinal sin. Then in 1637, along came Descartes, famous for his quote, "I think, therefore I am." I believe it's more accurate to say, "I am, therefore I think!" Descartes maintained that only humans have souls, so animals can't really feel pain. He thus pioneered the practice of vivisection, which allowed live animals to be operated on for the purpose of scientific research—further objectifying the animal world.

In the 20th century, many others would openly disagree with this way of thinking. Darwin was one who challenged this view and demonstrated that animals had their own unique intelligence. Paradoxically, in the past century and even to today, animals have continued to be treated like objects, as having no soul or spirit, here mainly to serve humankind's needs and purposes. Yet these attitudes are slowly changing.

With the spark of ancient memory awakening in many of us comes a deep longing to experience the intimacy with the natural world that was a way of life for our ancestors, who expressed their gratitude for the gifts of the earth through continuous prayer, ceremony, and ritual. They appreciated that whatever you took from nature, you always gave something back, and you used every part of what you've taken. They knew that every aspect of life was infused with Spirit.

I invite you to experiment with making the kinds of connections with animal spirit guides that I've outlined in this Part One. When you do, trust the message that comes to you, whether it's clear and obvious or rather cryptic. If you don't understand what's being conveyed, ask that particular spirit animal for clarification.

Developing the simple skills required to receive messages directly from Spirit through the animals is nothing short of magical and miraculous, as you will see. Don't just take my word for it; give it a try! It will inspire you and enhance your life.

In Part Three, we will delve further into practices and other interactive ways to deepen your connection to the animal world. Until then, enjoy the fascinating personal tales of our Sacred Storytellers.

PART TWO

Personal Tales of Encounters with Spirit Animals

Maybe it's animalness that will make the world right again:
the wisdom of elephants, the enthusiasm of canines,
the grace of snakes, the mildness of anteaters.

—CAROL EMSHWILLER

GRASSHOPPER SPIRIT AND THE JOY OF SONG

t was my dream guitar: a Martin D35 acoustic. The $700 price tag was a lot of dough for a 16-year-old (my age at the time). So, I worked a job and saved my pennies. Finally, the day came when I got to take this instrument home with me. It became my baby.

For the next couple of years, I had so much fun teaching myself various chords and fancy finger picking. Soon, I knew enough to play a few folk songs and some of my favorite rock anthems like Neil Young's "Cinnamon Girl" and Bob Dylan's "Like a Rolling Stone."

Singing is something I've always had an affinity for, as well. I've got a decent voice but was always so shy about singing around others. In private, I had no problem belting out "Hotel California" or humming James Taylor tunes, but when it came time to sing anywhere outside of my bedroom, I'd get very nervous. I had to force myself to overcome my shyness.

When I was 23, me and a friend, Bill, who I often jammed with, decided to co-write some songs. We had become friends with a fellow who owned a recording studio, and he was supportive of us and our music. So off to the studio we went to lay down some tracks. This experience helped Bill and me feel a lot more confident and relaxed in our talent. From there, we started performing at small venues around town. It was a blast.

We had no particular goal, though I did secretly fantasize about becoming a famous rock star. What teenager doesn't? In all honesty, I didn't think I had the ambition or talent to pursue music as a career. It was mainly for fun, an avocation.

We kept a band together for a short while, but my rock-and-roll dream faded with age and the distractions inherent in trying to be a responsible adult. Music continued to be an important part of my life, though. I stopped performing, writing, and recording, but I never completely stopped playing.

Then a few years ago, something took hold of me. Four years had passed since I'd picked up my instrument. I dusted off the Martin D35 and started strumming a bit. Soon I felt inspired to dig out and rewrite a couple of those older songs that Bill and I had created, and to compose some new ones.

For a few weeks, I was increasingly swept up in a delightful fever of lyrical and musical creativity. My passion returned with a joyful fury. I had forgotten about the sheer fun of simply playing and singing, let alone the thrill of writing some original songs. I followed the inspiration, excitedly picking up my guitar every day, and ended up writing quite a few new melodies and lyrics.

Before long, I had several tunes in final form and was excited to share them. Now that I was older, I was creating something that wasn't just for myself. I wanted these new songs to express something meaningful and hopefully stir something in the listener. I had an intuition that what was coming through me was that powerful. As I composed each one, it felt more like I was transcribing them from some other source or dimension. Clearly, they were guided by some higher force, as music often is, and I was the willing vehicle through which the songs showed up. In essence, I let the songs find me and come through me.

After playing them for my wife and friends, they encouraged me to share my new playlist with others. Over the next couple of months, I performed in a couple of coffee houses and received very positive responses. Before I knew it, others were encouraging me to record my compositions.

I attempted some home recording but realized that I needed to go to a professional studio to get the high-quality sound that I wanted. Since I hadn't been in a studio for years, I was nervous about it on many levels, but in spite of my trepidation, I set up a recording date for the following day.

The minute I made that appointment, fear started to creep in. I began questioning, *Are my songs good enough? Is there a real purpose in recording them?* Paradoxically, my gut was telling me that recording and producing them was important, and some inner muse was the driving force to do so in spite of my trepidation.

You have something to say through the music, it encouraged. *Have no fear.*

And yet, being only human, I did.

Later that day, I was sitting in my office, enjoying the balmy weather and light breeze wafting in from the open sliding glass doors. In anticipation of my studio appointment, I organized the songs I wanted to work on, feeling both nervousness and excitement.

The critical voice of the ego kept popping in and out, saying things like, *What do you think you're doing? Who do you think you are?* Yes, my internal critic was cautioning me to not take a chance, stay safe, not put myself out there. It's interesting how when we stretch our comfort zone, there's typically a part of us that doesn't want us to take risks, yet always opting for safety and comfort leads to a sort of death, doesn't it? The death of one's creative soul, at the very least.

As I was contemplating all this, a huge grasshopper jumped from the outside and landed squarely in front of my computer. I hadn't seen a grasshopper for years, and now here was one plopping down right by me. Staring at this tiny being for a few moments, I thought, *Okay, Mr. Spirit Animal guy, what does grasshopper mean?* I did what I first advise others to do when having an animal encounter: I asked for a direct revelation from Grasshopper Spirit, which I perceived through my inner voice.

Grasshopper's immediate message was: *Take the leap!*

This made a lot of sense, of course, and alleviated some of my nervousness about going into the recording studio. Closing my eyes, I reached out with my mind and heart to Grasshopper Spirit and asked, *Is there anything else I need to know?*

Immediately, I was overcome with an endearing memory of sitting in my backyard on a summer's eve years ago, the sound of grasshoppers singing all around me as I gazed peacefully into the starry, moonlit sky. I can hear their sweet, lilting refrain even as I write this. The memory touched me very deeply, and I understood in my heart that Grasshopper Spirit was offering to align with me as a powerful ally and support for my very soul, and for what my soul was urging me to do, through music.

For outer-world confirmation of Grasshopper's message, and just for fun, I did a bit of online research about the meaning of grasshopper as a spirit animal. I learned that there are about 10,000 species and each has its own unique song. With a few exceptions, only the males can sing. During courtship, male grasshoppers take turns singing songs, competing to outdo each other for the attention of the females.

But what really jumped out at me (no pun intended) was this message: *One of the gifts these insects hold is the power of song and sound. Song is an ancient way to alter consciousness and communicate with our animal and spirit relations. Some Native American songs date back at least 20,000 years.*

Okay, okay! I got chills up and down my spine as I read this, as the message was so obvious. I couldn't back out of this music recording appointment even if I wanted to!

The next day, I recorded five basic tracks (guitar and vocals) of my songs. I'm pleased with the results and have since shared these recordings with the world.

To this day, when I take a walk through the park and hear grasshoppers singing in unison, I am reminded of how music is so vitally important to me personally, to us collectively, and I often feel inspired to go home and immediately pick up my guitar. Recently, I did just that and was working on another new song, struggling to find the right music for the lyrics that had flowed out of my pen. I played it one way, then another, but couldn't find the perfect tune.

Instead of getting frustrated, as I typically would have in the past, I simply called on Grasshopper Spirit. When I did, he reminded me of something I innately knew since that day when I dusted off my guitar and picked up writing and composing again. I heard very clearly, *Let the song find you* . . . and it did.

Dr. Steven Farmer

SHAMAN HORSE

My ears throbbed strangely as I entered the horse's stall. The atmosphere there reminded me of the sensation I'd felt when learning to scuba dive in my teens. The heavy vibration of being under 10 feet of ocean was like floating into a different dimension.

Bracing myself emotionally, I walked toward Jester's hung head. He suddenly awakened from his stupor and gingerly moved to meet me. The voice of his owner, Joyce, drifted toward us.

"It's funny, Jester hasn't been able to stand for days, and he got up just as you arrived at the farm," she commented.

Joyce's love and concern, coupled with her anxiety to do the right thing, rang out as if from a greater distance than the one I had just traversed.

Jester exhaled a velvety breath onto my outstretched hands. It awakened a stream of energy that instantly created a sharp tingling in my palms. As Joyce's voice receded from my awareness, I felt Jester's consciousness growing. I exhaled and said a silent prayer: *Please help me get this right.*

Jester sent me a strong wave of reassurance through my hands, which were now starting to swell and heat up. How strange it was to have an extremely ill horse sending me warm feelings of encouragement, when I was the one who had been hired as an animal communicator to help *him*. I decided to let Jester lead me.

Letting go of my illusion of control as a professional, I ignored Joyce's ongoing monologue about the veterinarian arriving soon, and refocused on the connection between Jester's nose and my hands. I asked it to expand so I could understand with my mind what my hands were feeling. It was as if I'd been standing in a pond and suddenly found myself caught up in a heavy surf. The energy shot up my arms and my heart flooded with Jester's feelings.

He radiated love with such purity that I felt I might cry. Jester reassured me that he was joyful to have my help and wanted me to stay calm. Oddly, despite my amazement, his deep calmness affected me. *I am meant to be here, to play my role,* I thought. *I am blessed to be in Jester's presence.* I waited for more from Jester, resisting the urge to pry and prod.

He sent me more love and suddenly an image flitted across my mind's eye: a young girl riding a much younger Jester. His sway back and grey hair were replaced by a proud stride and rich mahogany coat. The vision continued with a series of scenes: Jester jumping a fence with the girl astride, the two of them sharing an evening while he grazed in his field as, nearby, she watched from atop the pasture fence, legs swinging in the gangly manner of a preteen. His adoration for this girl included feeling protective of her safety while she rode. Like a devoted uncle, he saw her huge loving soul for the wonder that it was.

His sense of guardianship was something I could feel in my heart. *You are in the presence of a powerful being,* I thought. Jester was fueled by love and participated unabashedly in his relationship with this girl. The relationship was profound for them both.

The transmission of information continued to occur spontaneously, layering across my consciousness to form a story. *Would I be able to remember all of what I felt from him?* I reciprocated to Jester how pleased I was to be his messenger, and that I understood he wanted me to comfort those he was leaving behind. His life was complete, having embraced and been embraced by this family, especially the young girl.

Yes, thank you for coming to help them, he conveyed. *They are so afraid. I am dying.*

A wave of sadness hit me, immediately lightened by his next thought. *It's now my time since horses don't live as long as girls.*

Choked up with admiration for his noble love, I nodded and vaguely responded to Joyce's repeated questions.

"Is he in pain?" she asked. "Have we done all we can for him?"

"It's all wonderful and he's preparing himself to cross over." I responded.

"I should have the vet come then?"

In my heightened state, Joyce's questions hit me like battering rams. Afraid to break the intense connection with Jester, I was all too aware that doing so could end our session prematurely. Besides, his vibration evoked love—while hers, anxiety.

Bravely, I asked Jester the question on everyone's mind: "Do you want help crossing over? The vet is on his way, and all are hoping to speed you through the painful phase of crossing over. Jester, is that what you desire?"

He became very still and continued to breathe love into my hands, sending a wave up my arms that cascaded over my head and down my spine. His response shocked me.

He simply said: *I took it for the girl.*

I heard these words while seeing a vision of a girl in a hospital bed, her head wrapped in what looked like a turban. Though I couldn't recognize her face, I knew it was the preteen I'd been shown moments earlier. I stood in admiration, flowing love back to Jester.

Just then I heard the tires crunching on the driveway. Jester knew the time for a decision was upon him as the vet conversed with Joyce in the barn aisle.

"I hope he's been comfortable enough . . . We have exhausted all possible avenues . . . Remember, we have never seen a tumor of this type on the outside of a horse before . . . I wish I were here to help the old guy recover . . . I just don't know what it is we are even treating."

When Joyce explained my presence, the vet politely raised an eyebrow and asked me what Jester had communicated.

"He told me that he took it for the girl."

Behind me, Joyce gasped and cried out. Shivers shot down my back. Jester suddenly retreated his energy, and I knew he was tired from transmitting. Joyce leaned into his neck, sobbing her thanks. Between tears, she confirmed the meaning of the vision Jester had shown me.

Her daughter, Lana, had developed an inoperable brain tumor two years prior. She took a swift decline and stopped being able to speak. Hospice was employed to keep her comfortable. Then suddenly one day, Lana started to talk again. The doctors had never seen such a reversal. The tumor simply disappeared without treatment. Hospice was sent away and she eventually recovered.

The realization dawned on Joyce as we all stood in wonder, each of us trying to process what this meant.

"It was shortly after that when this tumor appeared on Jester's leg," she explained through tears. "It became the shape of a cantaloupe, eventually morphing into something that looked very much like a brain."

Wow! You don't mess around! I joked with Jester. *You give the girl a lifetime lesson on love, save her life, then restore faith to a mother and a man of science!*

Jester whinnied and seemed pleased with himself. By now, my emotions were all over the scale—a mix of bubbling amazement and joy chirping through my heart.

Then Jester prodded my consciousness with the idea that he would now like the man of science to help him leave his body. He needed to relay this message to his family so they would know that Spirit had graced them. Jester yearned to rejoin with the Life Force and leave his tired body behind. I, too, wished to join him as he flashed to me a vision of the peaceful love awaiting him on the other side. Warmth flooded through me, knowing that I'd been graced by this amazing being and marveling that Spirit had included me in this profound experience.

Laura S. Rowley

YOU CAN'T SLEEP WITH A BUTTERFLY

*M*y wife, Bobbie, was the first to spot the butterfly circling around the ceiling lights in the convenience store. No one seemed to notice or show any interest in rescuing it, but Bobbie and I are always rescuing creatures of all sorts. I kind of see it as an extension of my life's work as a doctor. If something or someone can be helped, healed, or saved, I'm all for it.

We'd stopped by this store on the Hawaiian island of Kauai to pick up some supplies for a weekend workshop we were invited to give. I was thrilled to travel there because I love the islands and feeling close to God when surrounded by mountains, the ocean, and the beauty of nature.

Several years prior, a cancer patient that I'd counseled told me that she was going to Kauai, where her mother lived, to resolve her difficulties with her mother, then die there. She accomplished all that she had hoped for and passed from this world feeling loved, complete, and at peace.

Being that my patient, whom I'd felt close to, died on the island, doing a workshop on the art of healing in that same locale attracted me even more . . . and that butterfly, well, it sure was attracted to us.

When my wife saw it fluttering in the store, she felt compelled to climb up on the counter and hold her arms open towards it. The butterfly reciprocated by flying over and landing on her hand. I helped Bobbie down and we walked out of the store with both our purchases and this beautiful insect.

Once outside, Bobbie extended her hand, expecting the butterfly to happily fly off; but it just sat on her hand even when she shook it. So, we climbed into our rental car and drove back to the hotel, where we again tried to release the butterfly in the parking lot. It refused to fly free. Instead, it settled on Bobbie's shoulder. So, up the elevator it went with us and into our room.

By our bedtime that evening, the butterfly had become like family, staying near us no matter what we did to get it to leave. Things started to become rather mystical and I truly began to feel that this insect could be the spirit of my deceased patient. After all, the butterfly is a symbol of transformation; its transition from caterpillar to butterfly mirrors life, death, and rebirth.

"Honey, you can't sleep with a butterfly," I said, pulling back the bed sheets and plumping our pillows.

Bobbie stepped onto the balcony for a few minutes then came back into the room.

"There. I brushed it off my shoulder," she said.

I chuckled.

"Look at your other shoulder!"

Yes, it had flown over to Bobbie's other shoulder.

By now, I knew this was no coincidence; my patient's spirit was joining us. We stopped trying to shoo the butterfly away and instead enticed it to drink some water we'd sweetened with sugar and placed on the bedside table.

We awoke the next morning with our newfound friend still on the table. I spoke to it through my consciousness: *I'd like to incorporate you into my workshop today as a symbol of transformation.* My idea was to have the butterfly climb into a paper bag then release it at just the right moment to reinforce the symbolism of what I'd be speaking about.

The butterfly went right along with my plan. After we drove to the outdoor workshop site, I carefully placed it in a vented bag. At nine o'clock sharp, I began my presentation and after discussing the symbol of the butterfly, transformation, and its relationship to life and survival, I picked up and opened the bag.

Right on cue, out flew the butterfly. Of course, everyone—except for me—expected it to hightail it out of there, but it stayed and circled overhead the entire time I was sharing the story of my patient.

I have many other experiences to tell about other patients I've counseled—including lifesaving ones—where creatures show up as a representation of a deceased loved one, usually because of what that animal meant in the life of their family member or friend who has passed.

As for the butterfly on the island, it circled around our workshop space from early morning through late afternoon. When I announced at five o'clock that the event was concluded, the butterfly—again, right on cue—floated up higher and higher into the clear blue sky and flitted away.

Bernie Siegel, M.D.

SERENITY'S MESSAGE

"Tap, tap, tap!"

The sound of soft rumbling echoes through the living room. Her large nails gently touch the yellow siding of the front window that overlooks the soothing high tide out in the bay. The jaguar's sleek, muscular body moves with grace from her current perch on the windowsill to the worn, beige, crocheted-blanket-covered couch below.

Purrs continue to permeate the room as her beautiful golden tones and the hypnotic pattern of her black-and-orange-layered rosette spots sprawl across the couch. Her tail sways to the tune of the wind chime that catches the saltwater breeze on the porch. I feel the calming vibrations of her rhythmic purrs on the wood floor beneath my bare feet. The floorboards creak and settle under my weight as I take a few steps towards the front door.

She licks her enormous front paws one by one and yawns, showing her sharp incisor teeth before catching my eyes with her own. Feet away, I can see the milky-white whiskers that adorn her proud face. Her eyes sparkle like a sunrise as she looks at me with curious interest. Nodding her head to one side, she observes my own nervousness and confusion.

In that moment, the purring changes to a snuffling from her pink, heart-shaped nose. With her powerful muscles flexing her front paws and massive chest, she straightens her body and sits upright, remaining still like a statue at a fortress entrance. With her eyes fixated on my motionless stance, her intense gaze moves back and forth from me to her body, once adorned, as when she first gracefully stepped into this sanctuary.

The snuffling becomes louder. I take one more step forward into the bright light that makes the tiny hairs of her fur glow with a golden aura. Breathing deeply, I silently pray for help and safety. Adrenaline fills my veins as I struggle to remain calm.

As if she hears my plea, *Do come sit with me,* she says, like a queen inviting me to a glorious garden tea party. The snuffling is replaced by the rhythmic purr that her tail dances to. With another deep breath, I cautiously move forward, step by step, and take my place with her on her new throne. Still locked on her golden eyes, my heart races. She sits calmly as sunrays shower our backs with warmth. I allow my thoughts to slow, pondering whether this royal guest has a name . . . "Serenity." She looks up with her golden eyes before I complete the thought.

Her purring continues, now matching the slower pace of my heartbeat. Serenity snuggles her huge head against my side as if she is a common house cat. Her graceful affection calms my soul. Loneliness and fear dissipate into the harmonious combination of the saltwater breezes, deep rhythmic purrs, and the chimes still dancing in the wind.

I close my eyes from these surreal surroundings for a moment.

Trust in the signs. I am Mother Jaguar, and you will heal and teach others. These words echo in my mind.

Slowly, the bright light from the jaguar's majestic entrance gradually fades. The warm oranges, yellows, and golds disappear into the quiet, peaceful darkness then shift to soft beams of light that bounce off the purple walls in my present-day bedroom.

Slowly fluttering open my hazel eyes, I push back my long, dark-brown hair, and sit up in both awe and disbelief of this vision and vivid dream. Reality floods back into my body as I look around the room. The warmth of the sun filters through the oak blinds, resting upon the journal and pen I had placed down before falling asleep. The soft, brown journal is still open to the passage I wrote the night prior:

Dear Spirit, please help me. I am heartbroken and do not know what to do next. I am open to your wisdom and guidance. What is my path forward?

I remember feeling so overwhelmed after my couple's counseling session that night and trying to get my young children to sleep later than usual. With sadness overflowing and the need to recenter my overanalyzing mind, I had turned on a favorite drumming meditation after journaling my thoughts. I dozed off amidst the drumbeats.

I reread my heart-filled request from the night before then write down jaguar's important message: *Trust in the signs.* As I close the worn journal, tears well up. I can still feel the sensation of her tail swaying playfully across my back.

Through Serenity, my hope was restored. Through her golden eyes, I found my path forward. Upon her regal throne, I learned to trust. If I am ever in self-doubt, I remember her wise words and wait for synchronicities to emerge, knowing I am never alone.

Tela Talise

MY POISON FROG TEACHER

*E*ach morning, as I left my shaman's hut in the rainforest, there he was on the path to my door—a rare, green-black poison dart frog—looking up at me with curiosity and expectation. After sighting him three days in a row, I had to accept that his appearance wasn't random. He was waiting for me, ready to meet me.

It is quite uncommon to see these frogs in the wild. How lucky was I to see one just outside my hut three days in a row? His colors were beyond spectacular: cool, mint green with splotches of black. I knew it was the same frog because I recognized his markings—a clear circle of black on his head and upper back, with a black figure eight on his right side. He seemed so delicate yet I knew that he was also deadly.

When I met my frog teacher, I was acting as shaman-in-residence at an eco-resort in the high mountains of Costa Rica. The nature guide at the resort seemed a bit perplexed when I told him about my multiple encounters with this rare frog. He cautioned me that the small amount of poison the frog possesses is enough to make a human heart stop beating. Like most poison dart frogs, however, the green-and-black variety only releases its poison if it feels threatened, and wild specimens can be handled, provided the human holding them is calm and relaxed.

So, on day three when I saw him waiting by my door, I stopped in my tracks and gave myself a spiritual whack on the head. *I'm a shaman, for God's sake.* Finally, I bent down to say hello. As I did, the little frog raised himself up and we met eye to eye. I felt the telepathic "hello greeting" that I've come to recognize after 30 years of communicating with all sorts of spirits, entities, and animals.

I thanked him for coming and he seemed excited to open a dialogue. I asked if he had a message for me. The frog implored me to communicate to the world that we have to care for our water. He expressed concern that the water is becoming too acidic, and explained how sensitive frogs are to changes in the water. He was adamant that he is (and all frogs are) experts on this subject and should be listened to and consulted. He cautioned that if humans are messing with the water by messing with the air, it is not a wise thing to do.

Expanding his ribs and swelling his tiny body, my frog teacher bowed then lifted his head, demonstrating how he breathes through his skin and assesses moisture in the air. The information from the temperature and composition of the water touching his skin helps him to make decisions and take action.

When I shared this teaching at breakfast that morning, it prompted a robust discussion among the resort guests and staff about how water and air pollution are changing Costa Rica. The naturalist in our group helped us to understand how lucky the resort is to be high up in the rainforest and how the constant rain helps to clean and purify everything.

Honored to have received this important message from the poison dart frog, I was hopeful that there might be more lessons for me the following morning. When I awoke on day four and reached my hand to open the door, I felt a mix of excitement to see my new friend and an anxiousness that he might not be there. I prepared myself for disappointment. Maybe he had already said all he had to say.

Glee and astonishment coursed through me when I saw him there on the path, waiting to interact with me once more. I sat down next to this rare amphibian and thanked him for the prior day's powerful message. He encouraged me to learn to breathe through my skin.

It's the best way to gather information, he conveyed, *way faster and more reliable than your eyes.*

I asked if he had another lesson for me.

Yes, today's lesson is for you personally. His tone was ominous. *It is about the poison we excrete.*

He went on to explain how he only exudes his poison when he feels threatened.

Just like you do, he said with the serious-and-knowing tone of a wise teacher who truly had me pegged. *When you feel threatened, you exude poison, too. It's not a physical chemical like mine but it is perceived by those around you just like poison.*

Wow, I thought, *this little guy goes right to the core.* In my coaching practice, we call this "dropping a truth bomb."

We eject this poison to drive away danger or kill a predator, he continued. *I don't think that is your intention when you excrete your poison, so be careful.*

I bowed my head and took his message to heart as he continued to teach me.

Sometimes, very rarely, you need to drive a predator away. When you experience certain emotions, you exude poison. People around you feel this poison and run away.

He paused, giving me a moment to let this sink in.

Perhaps it is time for you to figure out other defensive responses that don't excrete a deadly poison.

It took me a couple of days to feel comfortable sharing this wisdom with the guests over breakfast. After all, I was at this resort conducting ceremonies, rituals, and healings. Wasn't I supposed to be in the role of the wise one?

My frog teacher seemed a bit low when we met on the morning of day five. I thanked him for the personal poison lesson and honored his astute perceptions.

"How's it going for you?" I asked in an effort to lighten the mood.

I'm very tired but I wanted to make our morning meeting.

"What's up?" I inquired, feeling compassion toward him.

He thanked me for the love. *It's just that I was up all night transporting eggs.* I had assumed that my frog teacher was a male because his voice sounded masculine. Oops! I guess not! *I had to carry all of the eggs up into the tree. It took several trips. It's a long way for me.*

I felt empathy as I looked at those tiny legs and contemplated the effort it would take to climb a tree. With as much peace and calm as I could, I reached out my hand and my frog teacher hopped into my palm. I held my hand steady, the back of my hand resting on the path so she could jump off at any point. I proceeded to give my first and only (so far) frog reiki treatment.

I started to send her life force energy but she seemed agitated. I considered her small size and quickly adjusted the flow to a trickle. She stretched out in my hand, pushed her back legs out and reached forward with her front legs. My wise and powerful teacher's belly was skin to skin with my palm. After a while, she said, *Thank you, that was great,* and hopped off and away.

I related all of this to the nature guide, including my mistaking her for a him.

"No, you are correct," he laughed. "Your frog is a 'he.' In this species, it is the male who carries the eggs and tadpoles up into the canopy. The little ones mature in the water pooled in the bromeliads. Both parents guard the tadpoles while they feed on algae and small invertebrates that inhabit the pools. So, he would have been doing a lot of climbing trips through the night."

He reached for his tea. "You should probably wash your hands just in case."

The next morning, day six, I had to be up and out very early to meet a local Bribris medicine man. I didn't know if my frog teacher had waited for me on the path or not. I stayed overnight with the medicine man's family and returned to the resort late on the afternoon of the seventh day.

On the morning of day eight, there was no magical green-and-black poison dart frog waiting for me; but I later learned that on day six, even though I wasn't there, a couple of the guests passed by my hut on their way to breakfast to see if they could meet my frog teacher. Lo and behold, there on the path were not one, but two poison dart frogs, side by side.

I couldn't help but tear up at the thought that maybe he brought the Mrs. to meet me, and I wasn't there . . . and did she think he was crazy, telling her stories of talking to humans?

John Paul (Eagle Heart) Fischbach

HEALING FOR THE HORSES OF WAR

*D*uring my first session of a practice called shamanic, or ecstatic, journeying, I experienced a simple vision of a carrot and a group of horses that led to a profound journey through history and healing. At the time, I wasn't sure what this vision meant. Was I to volunteer at a nearby rescue that housed horses? (I did happen to specifically know of one.) Was I to feed one of the horses a carrot? I knew very little about horses and had, in fact, tended to feel fearful around them, even as I loved and respected them deeply as a fellow species of Earth.

During the journey, I stayed with these visions, not insisting on receiving "answers." As the awareness deepened, I understood that the communication was particularly about horses of war—their collective trauma, sacrifice, and innocence. What they were forced to endure with no choice in the matter. What they witnessed and experienced in both their own species and other species, including the humans to whom they often give their love and loyalty.

Mesmerized by what I was receiving in this closed-eye vision, I considered for the first time what horses had to go through in innumerable human battles and wars, how they were treated and utilized as a tool even as some soldiers undoubtedly loved their equine companions amid the horror that humanity was engaging in and perpetuating.

These horses wanted to be recognized. They had an utterly natural desire for their sacrifice and trauma to be understood, seen, mourned, grieved—perhaps most importantly, to be healed. In my journey, I saw that this tremendous, wretched, tragic collective trauma on the equine species remains unhealed. I had no idea how to help or contribute to that. The sense I got at the end of that first practice was "to be continued."

This practice and its message struck me at a deep level. While I love animals and find the harm that they undergo at the hands of humans painful, I had not considered in much depth the profound trauma of these "horses of war." How many of them died excruciatingly painful deaths? How many watched their fellow horses do so, or observed the similarly painful deaths of humans, including ones they specifically loved?

That singular ecstatic journeying instance shifted my consciousness. I felt a new and distinct connection with these horses, a simultaneous grief and recognition of their unhealed experiences. Truly altered by this perspective, I could not believe I had not been aware of it before.

The next time I did this shamanic practice, I received that the horses wanted me to perform a ceremony to honor them and facilitate their healing. Not for a second did I consider not accepting this invitation, though I admit a part of me felt some nervousness about it. While I had learned about ceremony in my shamanic practice, I had not led one and didn't know what it would entail.

As I pursued this idea of doing a ceremony for the horses, I felt less concerned about how I should prepare for it. The horses themselves seemed to be leading me, so I did not need to figure everything out. When the actual ceremony was to be performed, more details would simply come, and they would let me know what I needed to know.

The horses wanted it to be an outdoor fire ceremony in my backyard. I received a vision of myself lifting a horse skull above the fire. Acknowledging this vision, I respectfully explained that I did not have a horse skull and was not sure where I would legally or ethically get one. Was there any alternative that would work? My next vision was of a piece of pottery I had made a couple years prior in a raku pottery workshop.

One of the methods we used in that workshop involved removing a pot from the kiln at around 1,300 degrees Fahrenheit and carefully dropping strands of horse tail or mane onto the sizzling piece. The burning imprints leave jagged black lines on the white clay. I appreciated the horses' ingenuity of seeing this as an alternative way to honor them and felt deep gratitude that I happened to have made that horsehair piece.

The horses also impressed on me during my practice that they would like the ceremony to be held on the anniversary of a battle that had taken place somewhere in my local region. I found myself wondering about the date. I knew very little about the details of any war, though I was aware that there was considerable history surrounding the United States Civil War in my region, as well as the Revolutionary War. But when? What if a seemingly relevant date was eight or nine months from now? Did they want me to wait that long? Or what if it was only in a day or two; would I have time to prepare for the ceremony?

Unbidden, the thought came to me: *Just relax. Maybe it's a date like September 4 or something that's not very far away but not so close that you would be in a rush.* I found it interesting that a specific date had accompanied this notion. From then on, September 4 seemed to linger in my consciousness whenever I thought of the impending ceremony.

In my next practice session, I greeted Mother Earth and opened to any further information about the ceremony. I saw hay bales situated around the fire. I asked how many; the answer was *three.* I committed to procuring three hay bales then asked if there were any other objects that the horses would like present or represented. A vision of a horseshoe came to me, which I also committed to procuring, as well as carrots and apples, which all made sense to me. Then an image of sugar cubes entered my consciousness. *Sugar cubes?* I chalked that up to a strange aberration yet found myself pondering how sugar cubes might be connected to the ceremony. Those more familiar with horses would not find this as perplexing as I did. I recalled that my maternal grandfather had been a horse trader and breeder. My mother was pretty familiar with horses, so I texted her:

"Random question: Do horses like sugar cubes? Did you ever feed them to any horses?"

She responded: "Yes, they do. They gobble them up."

I set down the phone and Googled "sugar cubes . . . horses . . . United States Civil War." The first hit was an article about General Lee and his horse Traveler—and how Lee "gave the horse sugar cubes." The second hit was an article about Rienzi, the war horse of Union General Sheridan, that included the line, "After the war, the nationally beloved horse undoubtedly got lots of pats, apples, and maybe sugar cubes from veterans and adoring fans."

I paused for a moment, feeling a little stunned by what was coming through me. Sure, things coming clearly and easily that made relative sense to me was one thing; receiving accurate information that was not part of my lexicon or conscious awareness was something else. While I harbored no skepticism about the existence of such a phenomenon, I had not often experienced it myself. It represented a trust and honor I was not accustomed to, and the profoundly humbling and sacred nature of it required some conscious sitting with.

A few days later, I began to address the question of the ceremony date. Because my particular area had a more prominent history with the Civil War than the Revolutionary War, I discerned that the Civil War would be the one to provide the battle and anniversary date for the ceremony. It was late August, and as I recalled the random date of September 4, I wondered if that date was given because it would indeed be convenient, given that it was coming up so soon.

I had no idea how to even start finding what battles might have taken place close to my area on what dates. Being as specific as I could get, I searched online for "United States Civil War Berryville Virginia." (Berryville is the tiny Virginia town—population 4,000—where I live.)

I didn't even need to click the link of the first hit to see the words offered in its preview: "The Battle of Berryville was fought September 3 and September 4, 1864, in Clarke County, Virginia."

Astonished by the actual significance of this date, I knew immediately that the ceremony would be on September 4. By that day, I had everything arranged in my backyard, including a semi-circle of three carefully placed hay bales with apples, carrots, and sugar cubes atop each. I took one apple and set it near the site as an offering to the honorees. The horseshoe and horsehair pottery piece were also carefully placed in the circle. As I lit the fire and opened this sacred ceremony, I did my best to convey to the horses my willingness and desire to facilitate their healing and that I would be honored for them to accept my invitation.

For the remainder of the ceremony, the horses guided me through my intuition, just as they had promised. Every part of it felt sacred and profound. At some point, I got a message from them or from Horse Spirit in general: To them, it didn't matter what humans were fighting about or which side "won." Could it not have been figured out without the wreckage that was perpetuated—on the humans, on other species, on the Earth, on the energy of life and existence? Whatever the pursuits or motivations of the various wars that humans had fought astride them, the horses themselves were a collective form of tragic collateral damage; not only that, but this damage was rarely acknowledged or recognized by human studies of history.

I concluded the ceremony by stating my hope that I had sufficiently honored the horses.

The next morning, I went out and reverently walked around the ceremony site, still feeling a bit unsure about whether I had done justice to this ritual that I was entrusted to carry out. It felt powerful, but did it help to facilitate their healing?

Wandering away from the ceremony site and further into the backyard, I was compelled to turn toward a large maple tree. When I did, a nearby object caught my eye. It was the apple I had left as an offering, stuck between the top of my wooden fence and the adjoining wire mesh used to contain my dogs' attempts to scale said fence. Amid the backdrop of pale wood and dark tree branches, the vibrant red was unmistakable.

I walked slowly toward it. In truth, squirrels often frequent my yard, and a squirrel is capable of carrying an entire piece of fruit. This would explain the apple's location, as though it had been dropped mid-climb. That didn't preclude, though, the section of visible white flesh where squirrels had undoubtedly munched through the shiny skin from looking like a much larger animal had taken a bite from it. Nor did it negate my having felt inexplicably drawn to that tree at that moment to see the apple in its resting place.

Whether my ceremonial offering achieved its intended effect or to what degree, I didn't know—and I felt content in not knowing. I went about my day, pondering if this leg of my journey through history with the horses was complete. When I walked back out to the yard that afternoon, the apple was gone.

Emily McCay

THE CAT, THE COYOTE, AND THE CROWS

Hearing the crows' frantic warning from inside the house, my intuition urged me to go outside. As I opened the sliding door to the deck, I saw a flash of motion near the fence that borders my property. Time slammed to a halt. A few yards in front of me, a large coyote had Lulu, my 17-year-old tuxedo cat, by the neck and was preparing to carry her away for breakfast.

I wasn't going to let that happen. Like so many other devoted pet parents, I am fiercely protective of my cats. There can be no greater horror for a pet owner than seeing one's beloved fur baby dangling from the jaws of a hungry predator.

Kahlua—or Lulu—is my youngest. My other two beloved cats—Tequila and Samrat—lived to be 12 and 14, respectively. I was able to fulfill my greatest wish of being there for them when they crossed the rainbow bridge. As Lulu aged, she had developed arthritis in her hip joints and hypothyroidism, but was pretty sturdy. Because of her limited mobility, she wouldn't venture far from the back door and wasn't able to jump the fence. I had no idea that coyotes could, though; I had never seen coyotes in my neighborhood.

As the crows watched all of this play out between my cat and the coyote from their vantage points high above the yard, I had the strange feeling that they somehow knew my story and that my three cats were treasured family members. At times over the years, I even thought I heard them caw their approvals.

I know that animals, whether in spirit or physical form, come into our lives for various reasons—sometimes, to save ours. I knew this partly because I've studied shamanic practices and had begun travelling regularly to Peru to train as a jungle healer's apprentice.

Two days before an extended trip to South America, I had reserved a spacious window suite for Lulu at my trusted boarding facility. We did our typical morning routine; I'd open the sliding glass door and let her out to putter around the deck. That morning, as Lulu passed over the threshold, she turned and glanced at me. I returned to the kitchen to make some toast. That's when I heard the crows making a racket. My hair stood on end when I spotted the coyote.

I ran across the deck towards it, yelling and waving my arms like a crazed scarecrow. He dropped Lulu and glared balefully at me before leaping the fence.

The coyote had bitten through Lulu's neck and her back legs were limp. I scooped her up, gently placed her in her carrier and drove to the nearby pet emergency center. Once there, I babbled out my story as the vet techs guided me to a private room. The veterinarian came in quietly to discuss Lulu's case. Yes, she was still alive and had a chance to recover, but it would require a lot of time and money. The coyote's bite had hit a main nerve, which could only be restored through surgery.

"Even then she may not regain full use of her back legs," the vet explained. "She might also lose control of her bladder and bowels."

With only two days until I was to leave for my extended trip to the Amazon, I was in a quandary. I didn't want to make a wrong move. Given her age and other health conditions, I needed more information. I authorized a set of X-rays to be taken. They revealed several tumors in Lulu's lungs. Like my other two cats, she had developed cancer; three unrelated cats . . . three different cancers. What are the chances of that?

Lulu was heavily medicated but conscious and she recognized me. Her dilated eyes widened briefly as she voiced a silent meow. I asked her if she was ready to join Samrat and Tequila, and that, due to the cancer, I was ready to let her go. She blinked her acceptance and nodded slightly. Had the coyote attack not happened, Lulu's lung cancer would have progressed unnoticed and her symptoms might have been very bad. What if she slipped into the spirit world while I was out of the country and I didn't get a chance to say goodbye? I would have never known what happened and there'd have been no closure. Had the coyote actually done us a favor?

Although I cannot be sure, I've come to believe that somehow my cat, the coyote, and the crows made a pact with each other in a way that I could not possibly understand. Knowing she had limited time left, perhaps Lulu called in a predator's spirit to help her transition swiftly. Knowing that finding her partially eaten body would severely traumatize me, however, the crows agreed to intervene—resulting in a more acceptable, peaceful end. She no longer had to suffer and I got to say goodbye.

Because of the gift of the crows, I was able to fulfill my wish to be there for Lulu, as I had with my other two cats at the end of their lives, holding her as she passed. Being able to say goodbye was really important to me. Had the crows not alerted me to the predator in the yard, the end result would have been much worse. I owed them big time.

Yet this is not the end of the story. Sometime later, I experienced a weird twist that only Spirit could have manifested. I had been a jungle shaman's apprentice for several years, learning the rituals and healing practices of the Peruvian Amazon indigenous people. On arrival in Iquitos, I made my way to my teacher's camp and settled in. I was still grieving the loss of Lulu, but decided I'd work with the emotions in that night's ayahuasca ceremony. This I did, allowing the tears to flow as I remembered how my three cats had kept me alive during some of the worst moments of my life. I had been such a good cat mom. How could I have let Lulu down so badly?

Javier, my teacher, came over to see what I was crying about. I told him the whole story about Lulu's death and he nodded in understanding.

"You are sad because she has been a part of your life for 17 years," he said. "Now you must make new habits."

Appearing to be receiving some internal message, he became wide-eyed and continued.

"When you are able to let her go, she will become one of your spirit guides and return as the yana puma (black panther) to help you in your work."

I really wanted to believe this, so I worked hard over the coming months to let her spirit fly free. Eventually, I forgot about Javier's prediction until about a year later. I had led a group in a shamanic healing ceremony the night before, and now we were all sitting in a circle talking about our experiences.

When the talking stick was passed to one of the women in the circle, her story sent chills down my spine.

"I felt something behind me, like a large animal. I turned to see what it was and a very large black cat passed by me. It went up to the altar where you were and then it vanished."

After a moment, it hit me: it was Lulu! She had transformed into the yana puma and was now back with me. After getting over my astonishment, I told the group about the events leading to Lulu's death and transformation.

Since then, several others have seen a large black cat strolling through the ceremonial space. And the crows? I gifted them with a large bird bath and continue to give them treats and rewards. We now have a mutual understanding: They will patrol my property and warn me of dangers, and I will take care of them.

Judy Lemon

GUIDANCE FROM AN ORANGE MOTH

I lost my best friend to cancer in 2015. Her death almost destroyed me.

One morning, shortly after her burial, I walked towards the lake dock to watch the sunrise. My heart felt extremely heavy as I grieved her passing. Suddenly, I stopped in my tracks as I noticed a beautiful orange moth on the ground trying to fly. It was wounded; one of its wings was not moving.

Pick me up, the moth requested. So, I did . . . and at that moment, I felt my best friend's presence. *Take me with you to watch the sunrise,* she begged.

As I sat on the dock with this beautiful creature, I was overcome with gratitude for being able to feel my friend's presence. The sky was a work of art, with an array of beautiful colors reflecting on the sun-lit water—a breathtaking masterpiece from our Creator.

I sat in silence as the moth crawled upon me and stayed close to my heart.

Enjoy the view, she conveyed. *Remember to always look up at the sky, especially when you are feeling down. Stay connected to Spirit and pay attention to the many ways that messages are communicated.*

After savoring one of the most spectacular sunrises I've ever witnessed, I walked back home, still carrying the moth, as I decided to protect her until she healed and was ready for release.

I walked through the house and outside to the screened porch, gently placed the moth on the screen and went to the kitchen to prepare some tea. I checked on her often to make sure she was okay. As I was getting ready to sit on the porch with her and listen to her messages, I noticed a green lizard on the screen. I was fascinated, as I had never seen such vibrant green on a lizard.

I felt the need to do an online search about this type of lizard. As I read about the green anole lizard, my eyes widened and I felt a tingling down my spine. I learned that moths are part of this lizard's diet. My stomach clenched and my heart started to beat faster.

I ran out and stared in horror as the lizard went for the kill. I banged on the screen, which made the lizard drop the moth and scurry away. *What do I do now? How do I save her?* I wondered. I decided to put her in a potted plant, under the leaves, and create a fortress around it. I was vigilant the whole day, making sure that she was safe with no lizards around.

The next morning when I checked on her, she was still alive. It worked! I was so relieved and grateful. I said a silent prayer of gratitude and asked that she be kept safe while I was at work.

That evening, I could not get home fast enough. I went straight to check on the moth. I was so happy to see that she had crawled out of the pot and was on the table. *Soon enough you will be well enough to fly again*, I thought. Then I looked closer and realized in horror that the moth was filled with ants; only her shell remained. I broke down in tears, wailing as my heart broke all over again. *I am so sorry I could not save you*, I whispered.

At that moment, I caught sight of a garden statue that I had next to the table where the moth had landed—a statue of a butterfly with the word "hope" etched on it. *There is no hope!* I silently screamed as I felt the pain of loss.

Suddenly, everything got very still. I felt the spirit of the moth alongside my best friend. I stood there in silence for what seemed like an eternity. Then my best friend and the moth imparted this to me:

There is nothing you could have done to save us. Thank you for loving us and for your efforts to keep us safe. It was our time to go . . . and now it is time for you to release us, as well as yourself.

A wave of peace passed through me as I released my guilt from what I believed was my inability to save them. Now I knew: They were not mine to save. They were only mine to love.

Laura E. Gómez

WISE OLD OWL

Snuggled in my tiny studio on a peaceful night outside my home in North Battleford, Saskatchewan, I enter meditation and set the intention to meet my spirit guide.

Guided into a vision of a beautiful starry night, I hear the ocean lapping as I walk alongside a crystalline coastline of powdery white sand near the Gulf of Mexico. Next to the shoreline, hemmed in by palm trees and rugged cliffs, is a large boulder twice my height. I begin to climb it one step at a time, feeling its rough, sun-warmed edges against the soles of my feet and palms of my hands.

As I emerge over the rock, the salty air caresses my face and my hair flies freely in the wind. Standing tall atop the boulder, completely relaxed and enjoying the solitude, I gaze out over the turquoise waters of the Caribbean Sea. The waves glisten with moonlight as I listen to them crash against the rocky coves along the shoreline.

Totally at ease, I feel a presence behind me. I turn around slowly to see a figure in the distance walking towards me. As he emerges in the light of the moon, I see that he is wearing a headdress and leather loincloth. I cannot decipher his facial features but the energy of this spirit feels familiar.

Gracefully, he arrives atop the rock where I'm standing. I notice that his large headpiece is made of various types of feathered embellishments. My attention immerses upon one particular white feather with dark markings. In awe of this vision, I keep my composure so I won't be pulled out of the meditation before I can receive some sort of message or guidance.

Time seems to stand still. Silently, the figure extends both hands to offer a small gift, intangible yet visible. It's fluffy and white. I reach out to retrieve the object as the figure slowly disappears from my mind's eye.

Closing my meditation, I hear a loud *hoot! hoot!* which brings my awareness back to my tiny studio. *Did I just hear an owl?* Still tranquil from the meditation, I let the thought go. Then I hear the sound again—this time, loud and clear. There's an owl outside of the studio! My heart skips a beat and I've got goosebumps.

I push open the studio door, smacking it into the fence in the attempt to startle anything that might be out there. Poking my head out, I look down the driveway then up on the studio roof. I don't see or hear anything unusual. So, I decide to make a run for the house nearby. Once inside, I pull the door closed and peer through its window, hoping to catch a glimpse of this mysterious owl. I hear occasional hoots for the next few minutes. Is he on the other side of the yard? I dash to the back door to see if I can spot him. Feeling a rush of excitement, I scurry around the kitchen counter to the back balcony door and slowly open it.

I catch sight of a luminous snowy owl with dark markings throughout his round body and wings—similar to the feather that caught my attention in my spirit guide's headdress. The owl is perched among the bushy branches of a spruce tree, with one wing slightly crutched.

Wow! An owl in the backyard! He's beautiful!

Taking a deep breath, I step out onto the balcony. We make eye contact for a few seconds before he begins to shuffle and shift on the branch, preparing to take flight.

As the snowy owl lifts off, I walk across the deck, keeping him in my sight for as long as possible. I can hear the swoosh of his large, white-downy wings as he flies higher then disappears into the night sky.

I stand there in silence, shimmering in total admiration for this creature. My soul feels aligned with the peaceful, harmonious wisdom of the universe.

Katha Sager

CROSSING THE BRIDGE

When I was five years old, I announced to my parents that I was going to hold my breath until they bought me a pony.

"Hold away!" they responded, but I persisted with this request because my love of horses is inborn in me. I've always been drawn to them.

Soon enough, I was gifted with riding lessons and from then on, there was no turning back. For several years, I put in my time at a local stable, mucking stalls and leading trails, while wishing for a horse of my own to love. I was an extremely shy and awkward child, yet when I was in the presence of horses, we naturally understood each other.

Outside of the barn, life often overwhelmed me. I am an empath with psychic abilities but back then I was clueless, honestly believing that others felt things the way I do. Everyone around me seemed to flow through life with ease, and I had no idea how they did this. My life felt like a turbulent ocean. The constant onslaught of others' thoughts and emotions rocked me like gigantic waves. I struggled through my days, desperately trying to keep my head above water until I could escape to the comfort of the horse barn. Being there gave me peace.

Finally, when I was 10 years old, my wish came true. A horse of my very own! My loving parents, with the best of intentions, purchased exactly what I wanted:

a two-year-old, green broke, purebred Arabian mare. Anyone who knows horses knows that this is a potential recipe for disaster, but gratefully, in my case, the Divine intervened to keep me safe.

Me and my mare (appropriately named Sassy) had our moments, for sure. Her antics included rearing, taking off and flipping over backwards, but Sassy taught me how to ride. Through it all, she became my soul mate in horse form, my guide and savior. Sassy was everything I wasn't and everything I needed— wild and willful, always confident. With a heart connection and a depth of understanding that rarely happens in a lifetime, my bond with Sassy taught me how to navigate life with the same grace and determination that I envied in others. We were inseparable for 34 years, right up through the day she passed in the spring of 2018.

Sassy let me know when it was her time to go. Until that day, she was full of herself, running full tilt, as usual, to the pasture gate to greet me. She passed peacefully with little suffering. I was grateful for her easy transition but I lost a piece of myself when she left physically. Little did I know that she would become my guide in spirit and how much I would soon need her.

In the fall of that same year, I went into the hospital for what was to be a routine sinus surgery. Not much in my life is "routine." I had a fatal reaction to the anesthesia used in surgery; when the meds entered my bloodstream and hit my heart, I went into cardiac arrest.

My soul left my body and hovered above it. I watched panic and chaos erupt in the operating room as the medical staff desperately worked to revive me. My soul-self was captivated by a brilliant, white tunnel of light. I had the sensation of moving through time and space. Words can't adequately describe the feeling of unconditional love and grace that enveloped me. I was overcome with joy and peace. A deep remembering engulfed my being and I knew that I had left the physical world behind. As my soul completed its transition, I was greeted by loved ones who had passed before me.

Then . . . there she was . . . my beautiful mare, Sassy. I rejoiced in our reunion.

Filled with awe, my loved ones in spirit assured me that I was not meant to stay in this glorious place. I was to return to my body and the physical world with a purpose that would be given to me by God, our creator. Sassy would return with me in spirit, too. As my soul completed its heavenly journey, it popped back into my physical shell, like air being pushed into a space-saving bag. It expanded to fill my entire physical form. Poof! With that, I dropped back into my physical body. Slowly, I became aware of my surroundings and reoriented myself to being a spirit in a human body once more.

Physically, I was broken. The muscles of my heart were stunned by the event. My body was battered by the medical team's attempt to resuscitate me. I was later told that I was dead for four minutes.

Spiritually, those four minutes filled me with a renewed awareness and blessed me with the knowledge and insight of my Divine experience and purpose. I was forever changed.

Months later, after a lengthy recuperation period, I began the difficult and daunting task of healing my body. Once strong and fit, that identity had been stripped away. I felt hopeless and overwhelmed.

This is when Sassy stepped in to lend me her strength and determination. Healed and whole again, Sassy appeared as she was in her prime, only now her dappled gray coat shimmered with soul light. Still so proud and full of herself, Sassy's confidence eased my fears.

Time and time again, I felt my fingers wrap into her etheric mane as she accompanied me on my healing trail. When I felt as though I couldn't venture any farther, she'd rear up and remind me of my own strength and determination, while making a promise that I didn't have to travel this path alone.

To this day, I still see, sense, and feel Sassy brightly trotting beside me on my life journey. Her soft horse scent fills me with joy and her presence is a blessing. Through her, I've learned that the bridge to the other side is not one way. It is a beautiful merging point that connects us to Spirit, and Spirit to us. This heart connection to loved ones, both human and animal, is priceless and eternal.

Mia Rusinko

HAWK MESSENGER

was startled off my feet. The thing nearly hit my head! When I realized what it was, I looked around to see if anyone had noticed what had just happened. There was no one around, so I just continued on my way to work, feeling stunned and puzzled.

"Wow! A gigantic red-tailed hawk just flew so close to me that I had to duck out of the way!" I said in amazement to my co-teacher as we entered the school building. "It landed about 20 feet in front of me and then just flew off. It was enormous! It came so close that the wind moved my hair!"

My comments didn't get much of a reaction from her or the other co-workers who heard me describing my hawk encounter. I was somewhat accustomed to that, as the atmosphere at my job had been feeling strained for a while. I enjoyed my work when I was directly teaching the kids, but the school administrators and me didn't see eye to eye. Many of my colleagues had a negative mindset and were unwilling to entertain any innovative concepts that threatened their old ways of doing things.

About a week later, another hawk (or, perhaps the same one?) swooped down between the school building and a grouping of trees on the playground, where I was standing hand-in-hand with one of my students. We both noticed that the hawk had dropped a feather in its wake. I picked it up, brought it inside and placed it on the science table to share with the class, which they enjoyed.

At the end of the day, I decided to take the feather home with me. I had a sense that this bird was specifically visiting me at my place of work for a reason. I gently placed the feather over the visor in my car where I could easily see it.

That weekend, I traveled to visit my family. On the way, I reflected on how I was increasingly not feeling good about my work situation. Once there with my family, I shared about my encounters with the hawk. To my surprise, my sister pulled out a book on animal totems.

"The hawk is your totem animal," she said, opening the book to read about red-tailed hawks. Beneath a photo of two red-tailed hawks, the passage described them as messenger birds, and to pay attention whenever one shows up, as an important message is coming.

With this information, I found myself constantly surveying the sky and my surroundings for hawks over the coming weeks. Eager to be in the magic, I longed for another visit. To appease my fixation, I checked out books from the library about hawks and other raptors in my demographic area. I brought the books to school to share with my students. While I did spot an occasional hawk around the school that we could view through binoculars, about a month passed until I was once again up close and personal with one.

It was the beginning of June, a beautiful, warm spring day in western Massachusetts as the end of the school year neared. I had just taken my class indoors for a period of rest before the latter portion of the school day. The children rested quietly as soft music played in the dimly lit room.

Suddenly, a loud, startling screech permeated the tranquility of the space. The children's heads began to pop up in wonder. I looked with a raised eyebrow at my staff members as the screeches continued. Finally, I went to the door and caught sight of an amazing hawk perched on the chain-linked fence about 10 feet in front of me. It would not stop screeching, and screeching, and screeching, and it was beautiful.

Soon, my co-workers in the nearby buildings began to come out to see what the commotion was all about. Aware that my intimate moments with the hawk would be fleeting, I cautiously stepped forward one, then two steps. The bird and I stared at each other for several more seconds. As more people came onto the scene, it flew to a slightly higher perch, then higher, and higher still.

The staff corralled children back indoors and we resumed class. As my day transitioned into evening, I felt profoundly moved by the experience I'd just had. In the coming days, I obsessed about it, wondering, *What is this hawk saying to me?*

A couple of weeks later, as the school year ended, it all came clear to me. I needed to step away from my teaching career, and the hawk was screeching at me to do so. I was at an impasse with administrators and was no longer in alignment with the direction of the organization. Heeding this animal totem's advice, I requested a leave of absence and began my studies to become a holistic health counselor.

And so began the first leg of my spiritual journey and new career path. That hawk screamed at me until I pulled myself out of my former environment and into a new direction. Message received.

Chris Ciepiela

QUESTING FOR A VISION

"*L*ighten up, Tom," my vision quest supporter suggests. "You need to go into this joyfully and full of humor. Don't be so serious."

Our sacred quest in the Santa Cruz Mountains begins with a purifying sweat lodge ritual. Then we set off to spend a night in the majestic redwood forest, having fasted for five days leading up to it. A cluster of seven stately trees serves as a border between my circle and the dense forest—as if they are holding the circle. Next to the redwoods is a small log bench.

Early in the evening, I find myself sitting on the ground, back up against a tree, listening to what I first think is the singsong of a bird. I strain my eyes to see where this sound is coming from. High in the tree is not a bird but a squirrel, and it is not singing. It's laughing . . . yes, laughing . . . laughing up a storm of joy within me. It stays there for close to an hour until I am all laughed out.

Then I notice a parade of clouds through the tops of the redwoods, with outlines of humans and animals in all shapes and sizes. It brings back joyful, childhood memories of Thanksgiving Day parades. Jesus, The Buddha, and spiritual teachers, healers, and guides of all faiths float by. Whereas the squirrel had tickled my funny bone, these awesome clouds grab my attention in a most reverent and humble way.

At dusk, my eyes seem to play tricks on me. Gazing up one of the hills, I see what appears to be a group of animals hopping around with incredible playfulness. It is pleasant and a bit eerie at the same time.

Once the sun sets, the forest becomes very dark. The treetops overlap, blocking most of the stars and all of the moonlight. I am determined to stay awake but I eventually doze off. Around three o'clock, somewhere between awake and asleep, I roll off the bench onto a large pointed rock. Ouch! Now, I am positively awake and alert—and cold.

I put on my hooded sweatshirt and tie it tight around my face. Alone and stone sober awake, I convince myself, *I am not hungry. I am not tired. I am not frightened.* I wait patiently for the crisis that will produce the vision on this quest.

Ten minutes later, I hear an animal approaching. *I wonder if it is the two deer that I saw the day before, coming to visit me.* Its *thump, thump, thump* is not the sound of deer; this animal is larger and lower to the ground. I can feel its presence as it rounds the hill towards me. I instinctually know that it is not the least bit afraid of me. This is its forest and I am the visitor, not the other way around.

When it comes within a couple of feet, I notice that I am not afraid either. *This night I will either live or die*, I think.

Suddenly, the most spectacularly powerful energy rises from inside of me beyond anything I'd ever felt before. It encircles me like a protective shield, only I don't feel that I need protection. This internal power has a voice that connects me with the animal.

Friend, that is close enough, the animal speaks to me. *Sit a while and let us talk.*

The animal stops at the edge of my bench and sits on its hind legs. For a period of time, a surreal energy exchange takes place, a mystical conversation between the animal and me, like the bubble captions of a comic strip but without the written words.

At some later point—I don't know how long—the animal stands, backs up and saunters down the hill in the same direction which it arrived. In the morning, I return to the camp clear minded but with this experience seared in my memory.

Before our group gathers to share our visions, I do a quick online search to learn about the animals in the area. I discover that mountain lions are prevalent.

Six months later, a friend who was on this quest shares with me one of her visions from that night.

"I saw you wearing a hooded sweatshirt, pulled tightly around your face, sitting on a bench with a sharp stone underneath," she explains. "I could see particles of an animal's breath and your breath joining in a mystical way, like two clouds coming together as one."

Dr. Thomas C. McGarrity

PURE JOY

t was a cold, overcast afternoon in February as we passed through the Roosevelt Arch at the northern entrance of Yellowstone National Park. Clouds clung to the horizon and melded with the snowcapped mountains. Elk and bison were the first to greet us.

We remained focused on our goal, as the days are short during winter months in Yellowstone. A lingering thought prevailed: *Would this be just another day in my 22-year-long dream of seeing a wild wolf?* Our anticipation was as high as the expectation.

Passing through the town of Mammoth, we followed the only road open to car travel and headed east. Soon, a group of four people on the side of the road came into view. They were standing on a snow-covered pullout, each with their own spotting scopes, focused on a distant mountainside. We knew that we had to stop, as there was little doubt what they were looking at.

One of the couples was German and, like most wolf watchers, they were more than generous in sharing their observations with other curious onlookers. Their thick German accents lingered in the crisp air as the woman invited me to step up to her scope. As I gazed through the lens, there before me was my first glimpse of wild wolves—a big, beautiful black male lying regally in the snow and a gorgeous, graceful gray female sauntering up to greet him. They met nose to nose, briefly making a loving gesture to one another. They were the alphas of the pack.

In that nose-to-nose moment, emotions began to unexpectedly swell deep inside of me. I stepped away from the scope, hardly believing what I had just witnessed. Two wild wolves in their natural habitat being free to be wolves! I looked at the German woman, who towered over me, seeming as tall as a grizzly in her oversized winter coat.

"Oh my gosh! You just showed me my very first wild wolf!" I blurted out. "I am *so* going to hug you!"

Without hesitation, she opened her arms to invite me into a long, grateful bear hug, 22 years in the making.

Our gracious hosts kept encouraging us to look through their scopes. They informed us that there were 10 wolves in total and they were called "the eight-mile pack." The beauty and grace of these creatures was magnificent. While gazing through a separate scope, we spotted three other wolves walking in the snow, slowly moving up the mountain to greet the other two.

Overflowing with excitement, I stepped away from the group and did a happy dance right there in the middle of the turnout, while silently rejoicing in my head, *We saw wolves! We saw wolves!*

As the others smiled at my unbridled display of excitement, happy tears began to slowly cascade down my cheeks. Seeing the wolves truly touched my soul. I had no doubt that this is what pure joy feels like.

Anyone who spends time in nature knows that magical moments are inevitable. How these experiences will ultimately affect us is unknown. That day, watching these incredible animals being kind, affectionate, and thoughtful to one another was a blatant reminder of how mankind is supposed to be. I knew that my life would be forever changed by having this brief yet powerful encounter, and that I would carry with me this reminder to always be more present and respectful. In those moments on the mountain, the energy of the wolves merged into mine and a long-ago connection was rebirthed. I felt the bond that holds the pack together, for we—just like the wolves—are only as strong as those who follow in our footsteps.

We continued to observe the pack meandering about the mountainside and mingling as a united family, as if they didn't have a care in the world—such a contrast to the reality of their existence, especially outside of parks like Yellowstone. Perhaps that is what drew them into the park.

Then they wandered into the trees and, just like that, they were gone. Alas, the world suddenly felt a little less wild again.

Karen B. Shea

FLOATING ON A STINGRAY

The cricket on my suitcase chirped in a fortune-telling tone: *Anything can happen.*

I took this message seriously as I kept packing. It was the day before my 44th birthday and we were headed to the beach in California. Just thinking of the sweet smell of the ocean and calming touch of the sand gave me a feeling of magic.

After a long drive, we were finally at the beach having a joyous time dancing, playing, and laughing. At five o'clock that afternoon, my daughter and I decided to run into the ocean waves one last time before returning to the hotel for dinner with the rest of our family.

Holding hands, we ran full speed into the water, our legs strong, our laughter contagious. Then, out of nowhere, I went down in severe pain. In an instant, my body hit the sand bottom under the waves.

Ouch! I must have stepped on glass, I thought.

In excruciating pain and weak in the knees, I slowly crawled to the shore. Within minutes, my body was shaking and in shock. I could barely breathe, let alone walk, but I managed to get myself and my young daughter back to the hotel room to call for help.

I soon learned that my foot had been gashed by a stingray tail and its venom had entered my blood and lymphatic system. For the next few hours, I stayed in bed with my foot elevated, exhausted and still in pain, and tried to calm my nervous system.

Around one o'clock in the morning—either half asleep or halfway to another world—I entered a state of pure bliss beyond anything I've ever experienced. Colors, tingling, pricks and other sensations moved throughout my body. I was aware but my mind was blank; it seemed to be connected to a precise point in time and space yet, the point expanded and contracted. My body felt featherlike and luminous, vast and cosmic. In this beautiful, fluid space, it was as if I was one with the ocean and all of its dynamic life—including the stingray that gashed me.

Hold on tight and come with me, the stingray said to me in these surreal moments.

There I was on the stingray's back, floating through the water in the most delicate and effortless way. I felt the ocean's essence as etheric and blissful.

As we swam together, I sensed the stingray's pride in his beautiful home. He allowed me to morph into him for just a second. It was as if the speed of our swimming created the frequency for us to become one. I felt his pulse, his desire, his freedom, his gracefulness. I went beyond any concept of having pain or a physical body. Then suddenly, the stingray was gone.

I opened my eyes to get my bearings and comprehend what had just happened. My heart had burst open into a state of grace.

Then the pain in my foot returned, making me aware that I still had a healing journey ahead of me. In the coming weeks as the wound healed, my encounter with the stingray continued to awaken parts of me that needed to surface and be reborn so that I could become a stronger version of myself. The physical healing was also challenging because my immune system had a heightened response to the incident, which triggered autoimmunity issues and an infection.

I reached out to a shaman friend for support. I had not shared anything about the stingray, just that I'd had a rough couple of weeks.

"A friend brought this to me and told me that someone I knew would need this," he said when we met. He looked deep into my eyes and seemed quite serious. "I think that person is you."

As he reached out to give me this gift, I noticed a cricket on the floor, reminding me of the cricket's message before my trip to California: *Anything can happen.*

My friend handed me a long, red velvet pouch.

"Go ahead, open it," he said.

Inside was a magnificent, ivory stingray tail, completely intact and with captivating sacred geometry. Tears came to my eyes, as I knew my stingray story wasn't over.

"Meditate with the tail and call upon stingray medicine as needed," the shaman suggested.

I came to understand that my experience on the beach that day had a much larger meaning. What happened to my immune system became part of my spiritual journey and uncovering my soul's purpose—to connect with nature, the deeper parts of existence, and to learn to embody all of these teachings.

Now, the stingray tail has a special place in my heart and on my altar. I use stingray medicine to heal and enhance my immune and nervous systems. It facilitates my connection with the healing energies of the sea. I now understand that the fluid systems in our bodies are very similar to those of the oceans and the stars. The etheric light that inhabits all of Creation speaks to us and acts as a "glue" to maintain order and cohesion.

We are not just part of this equation. We *are* the equation to the totality of what we as humans cannot name. As we learn from nature and other dimensions, we become more of the Creator's "dream", expressing in this third-dimensional world. I have learned that this dream uplifts, heals, leads to wholeness and balance and, most importantly, honors all of life.

Stingray medicine has shown me that we are more than our fears and thoughts. Like the ocean, life holds the mysteries for each of us to become abundant and infinite. This vast, multidimensional oneness is available to us every moment. Through stingray, this experience of oneness—its ecstasy and power—has given me a new outlook on life.

Tamara Knox

FRED THE SNAKE

*T*he morning sunlight streaming into the kitchen is dazzling, but not so bright that I cannot see him clearly.

Oh my God, what's he doing inside?

I feel a strange dichotomy of fear and eerie calm in the presence of the nine-inch-long, poisonous snake curled up inside my windowsill.

Instinctively, I reach for my cell phone camera and click a photo. My heart is pounding, and I'm absolutely certain that he is here for a reason other than to startle me. A jumble of thoughts and emotions rush through me at once. I feel an urge to reach out and touch him, to make sure he truly is real.

In the midst of my hesitancy, he moves slightly. Though logic says that snakes cannot talk, I get a distinct sense that he is speaking directly to me.

You know I won't harm you in any way, he tells me.

I open the back door while not taking my eyes off him, then quietly grab a pair of kitchen tongs. I sense an increasingly steady calm emanating from him as I place the tongs gently yet firmly behind his head.

"I know you won't hurt me and I won't hurt you either," I say aloud. "But you don't belong inside the house. You'll be happier outside, so go."

With that, I gently fling him loose from the tong's grip. He scurries off in the grass and I go back inside, my heartrate returning to normal.

Later, I get the impression that "Fred the snake" had delivered his message for me and wouldn't be back. A huge part of the message was about change—specifically, that much in my life will change, or needs to change. Hearing and sensing this, I see a quick yet horrifying vision that thankfully leaves my mind quickly; only a stark sense of terror is left. Yes, there will be change, there needs to be change.

I never saw Fred again but his message remained firmly planted in my consciousness, and I sensed that all will be well in the end.

About three months later, as I step off my glassed-in front porch, there slithers another black snake. It is not the only black snake I'd seen on my property, but never had one come right up the house steps.

Hello, he says, bringing a smile to my face.

I know this species is called a rat snake; he's non-poisonous, and longer and slimmer than Fred. I snap a quick photo then rattle the door, which causes him to slowly glide away as the sun glints off his back.

If Fred had stirred a message in me, this snake is here to remind me of it. I feel a sense of relief that although some change had occurred and more was coming, these changes are bringing improvement. I may not know exactly how or when or why. I only knew that what was transforming in my life is for the better—and that, in some ways, it already *was* better.

"What is your message for me?" I ask the snake before he disappears into the yard.

You'll know. Just be who you are. Be still and remember me, and you will know.

I take in the message as I watch him slither through my flower bed. With the sweet fragrance of peonies and lavender in the air, I smile, relaxed and happy in knowing that all is as it should be.

Eileen Love

CROW MEDICINE

a cacophony of cawing and squawking suddenly interrupts the quiet winter day and draws me to the window. Troubled with coughing and dizzy spells, I had been resting at home on the couch, but now I'm wide awake. As I peer out the window, a cloud of crows, far more than I can count, darken the sky and fill the branches of the maple trees that line my street.

My yard, previously blanketed with pristine white snow, had turned into a moving sea of black. I am mesmerized by the frenzied hubbub, the landing and taking off and landing again. Then my breath pauses as I realize that the other lawns in my neighborhood are still white, the other trees, still bare. I know beyond doubt that all of this commotion, all of this chaotic display, is for me.

A large flock of crows is sometimes called a "murder", perhaps because they have long been considered an omen of death. I feel no fear, however; only fascination, delight, and wonder. To me, crows are messengers from Spirit that capture my attention.

From that day forward, crows continued to make regular appearances at my home. Each day, a few would come to check out my offerings of food, then strut around the yard like self-important businessmen in their sleek black suits.

Their comical yet dignified presence keeps me enthralled as I contemplate their purpose. What is their message?

Six weeks after the crows first arrived, my hand began to shake involuntarily, and I developed a one-sided headache. I had ignored the coughing and dizziness, but these new symptoms gave me pause. Did they warrant a trip to the emergency room? For years, my only doctor visits had been for annual checkups. That evening, I argued with myself. My next checkup was just a week away. Surely this could wait until then, but the cawing of the crows urged me to take action.

In the emergency room, tests revealed a golf-ball-sized brain tumor, which had metastasized from a previously undiscovered lung cancer. I was admitted to the hospital and scheduled for brain surgery as soon as possible. My out-of-town support group arrived the next day: my boyfriend, my brother, and a friend who communicates with Spirit as easily as I can pick up the phone. Her spirit guides had kept her up all night, sending her to be with me.

From my hospital bed a mile from home, I could still see crows daily, flying overhead or perched on the vantage point of a tree or building. By now, I regarded them as old friends, and their cawing brought me comfort.

A few days after surgery, my boyfriend, brother, and friend nestled me into a wheelchair, bundled me up in blankets, and took me onto the hospital grounds where the snow had now vanished under the sun's rays. Grateful for my life and for this time with loved ones, I inhaled the fresh hope of spring.

As my boyfriend carefully rolled my wheelchair over the bumpy lawn, I took in the greening of the grass, the buds on the trees, the birds singing. A woman passing by noticed my bandaged head, looked into my eyes, and gave an encouraging thumbs up.

And then the crows came. A small flock this time, cawing overhead, then landing in the surrounding trees and on the ground, cawing back and forth. Again, I knew they had come because of me. This time, their message was loud and clear.

"They're telling you to not be afraid of the dark," said my intuitive friend. My vision blurred with tears as I opened my arms to the sky, to the crows.

A week later, I returned home with a walker, still too weak to take care of myself. My support team stayed to help. Every morning, I shuffled into the living room and looked out the front window. Often, several crows would be there, but always, a lone crow kept watch. He'd march down the sidewalk, back and forth, back and forth, reversing direction each time he came to my property's boundary. Sometimes another crow would give my sentry a break, and with a seamless changing of the guard, the new crow would take over where the other left off. The crows continued their constant watch until my strength began to return.

Nine months later, my boyfriend, now husband, made a beautiful hand drum for me for Christmas. The leader of his Blackfeet Sun Dance lodge painted it with an illustration of one of their legends about crows. It's a story of a time when darkness covered the earth. Without light, the plants withered and died, causing great hunger and sickness throughout the land. In desperation, the people sent a young boy to search for the crows and seek their help. They believed that because of the crows' love for shiny things, they would know where the sun and the moon were hiding. With the help of the crows, the sun and the moon were found, light returned to the earth, and the health of the people was restored.

Many other cultures, including Celtic, Inuit, and Chinese, also have legends of crows bringing light to the darkness. In these stories, the crows are messengers from another realm that serve as a bridge between light and dark, life and death. Once I was introduced to the legends, the crows became, more than ever, my symbol of hope. They have continued to be there for me ever since their initial appearance. No matter where I am or what I am doing, not a day goes by without the appearance of a crow. I know they are bringing the support of the universe, just as they brought light back to the people in so many legends.

Believing that my healing depends on mental and spiritual work, as well as physical, I employed visualization and prayer along with chemotherapy and radiation. And I used my favorite medicine of all: the medicine of the crows.

I shed my old name, as a snake sheds its skin. It was time for a new last name, a name with the power to heal behind it, a name of my own choosing. It was time for a name that could dissolve the darkness with light. It was time to become Kathleen Crow.

Katheen Crow

MY EMOTIONAL SUPPORT SHARK

was nearly four years old when the blockbuster movie *Jaws* aired on television in 1979. I remember my mother covering my eyes during some of the scariest parts; even so, I became afraid of the open water. Admittedly, this led to many thorough inspections of public pools before deciding to swim in them, and I was certain that I would never risk swimming in the open ocean.

As a young child, I felt greatly misunderstood and often overwhelmed with feeling the emotions of others. Sometimes my heart hurt by caring for humanity and the Earth so much that the insensitivity in the world felt unbearable. The only way I knew how to survive was to find a way to shut down or develop a thicker skin. I needed help, which came to me through an unlikely journey.

Gradually, the fear that sharks could be lurking in virtually any body of water lessened as I grew up, but I would occasionally have nightmares about being attacked by them. Then one night I had a powerful dream that completely changed what sharks represent in both my inner and outer worlds. In the dream, my life was in danger as I was held hostage on a boat captured by pirates. My hands were bound behind my back, but I could see an open door leading to the bow. I had to act quickly to save my life. Bolting out the door, I dove into the ocean where sharks were circling. The pirates crashed into the water after me. To my surprise, the sharks attacked my captors but did not harm me. When I awoke, I realized that sharks, as a dream symbol, had just transitioned from predator to ally.

My dream encounters with sharks continued. In another one, I was standing near the edge of a swimming pool with a great white shark swimming in it. A wave of fear engulfed me, but being able to just watch the shark up close allowed some of that fear to dissipate. Without this fear, the shark before me was not like the killing machines they were portrayed to be in *Jaws*. In fact, it felt as though the shark had deliberately appeared to connect me back to my childhood fears, as a way of meeting that younger part of me. Something about this connection felt personal, as if this shark knew me.

The next step in my journey happened while visiting the Big Island of Hawaii. My friends had taken me to several snorkeling spots, and I was excited to try it for the first time. By then my trepidation of open water had waned but a fear of sharks still lurked in the back of my mind. I flashed back to all the times I had watched *The Undersea World of Jacques Cousteau* as a child, wishing I could break through my fear and explore the oceans. Here was an opportunity before me to finally overcome it.

The water temperature in the bay was perfect that day—warm near the surface and cooler down below. I had never before seen such beauty under water. So many colorful fish! Being surrounded by other snorkelers made me feel safe, so gradually, I ventured farther out. As I swam away from the rocky shore, I was surprised at how clearly I could see to the ocean bottom. Excited by the vastness before me, I continued swimming until I couldn't see the bottom at all. Instead, my vision became filled with the most magnificent display of wavering lights. Gradually, I saw less and less colorful fish, but I felt more and more connected to the Earth and to my soul. This was a moment with God that I could not let go of, and that would not let go of me. I kept swimming into the great unknown.

When I finally looked up to see how far I was from shore, I was surprised and a little alarmed. For a moment, I started to panic. I was alone in the open ocean, but then I did something magical. I just floated, face down, watching the dance of the sun's rays penetrating through the deep blue sea as I surrendered. I was overcome with peace and wonder. The only shark I felt in my presence was the great white from my dreams, letting me know I was safe. In those moments, I let go of my subconscious fears and allowed the Earth to receive me in a new way.

Elated by this rebirth experience, I swam back to shore and invited my friends to join me. Together we swam back out and floated together, holding hands, entranced by the wonders of creation. By the time we returned to shore, I felt more in touch with my inner child, the adventurer.

Not long after this snorkeling experience, I dreamt about swimming in the ocean again, but this time the great white shark was nearby, and I was not afraid. I began to feel a more intimate connection to this being, which seemed to be journeying with me for some mysterious reason that I didn't fully understand.

I was now ready to face my fear of feeling the oceanic depths of my emotions, to reclaim the gifts that had been displaced in the troubled waters of my childhood. I requested the support of a facilitator to guide me through a process of reconnection.

On the night before the healing session, I had an extraordinary vision that I believe was a memory of an out-of-body experience from early childhood. I found myself in the ocean at night, but I was not alone. I was hugging a great white that had come to me as an ally, while crying deep sobs of empathy for this greatly misunderstood creature. And the shark was equally empathizing with the gifts of a misunderstood child that could find no ally in the human world. In this memory, I was the same age as I had been when I first saw *Jaws*.

Then it hit me. Some 80 million people tuned in to watch that movie on television in 1979, but humans were not the only beings in the audience. Rippling throughout the world's oceans was an awareness of how sharks were being portrayed as monsters. Apparently, the sharks were experiencing how this movie was shifting humanity's relationship to them, and on some level the empathic part of me felt their anxiety.

In this out-of-body state, I became connected with a great white and felt its pain and sadness. We consoled each other, both crying that the human family had strayed so far from understanding our living connection to the animals and the Earth. I could feel how this shark cared for us, and its own kind, in ways that most people could not imagine. This connection, as it turns out, was a divine gift.

On the day of my healing session, my facilitator invited me to call upon any spiritual guides that I wanted to help me in the reconnection process. Without even having to think of it, the great white shark from my vision swam right into my heart. All at once, the memories came flooding in of the pact I had made with the shark. I had promised that I would help undo the misperception of sharks as vicious, soulless creatures. In turn, the shark would hold some of my empathic sensitivity until I was ready to retrieve it.

This shark had become my protector during a time when I felt unsupported by human beings. I burst into tears, and into my heart poured the missing emotional depth and sensitivity that I had not felt supported to embody by the human world. Only a creature this maligned by humanity could contain the depths of my sadness. The shark gave me everything I needed to begin the reconnection, right then and there.

The shark's spirit stayed with me in both my dream and waking states as I integrated more of my emotional sensitivity going forward. As I became more conscious of her presence, she continued to guide me, even in many practical ways.

I realize now how important it is to have allies on a heart level, so we can find our path to love courageously. As I opened to a greater ocean of being, I felt safer beginning that journey with help from my emotional support shark—the silent companion that has seen me through this healing journey.

Saryon Michael White

OWL ILLUMINATING THE DARKNESS

*M*y brother, Ed, gave my little girl a special book when she was four years old. Its luminous, pastel drawings illustrate the story of a boy with a secret friend. He and his friend rendezvous at night to roam the world of darkness that others rarely see. His friend is a snowy owl.

So many years have passed, but still when I open the first page of that book, I weep. The heart of the story, the bond between person and owl, is rooted in my soul.

In my twenties, my first husband, Dean, and I built a cabin off grid in the woods, where we raised our two daughters. One evening many years ago, just after dusk, I looked out the wide front window to see our neighbor pulling up the rough driveway in his van. He parked and walked to our front door with a bundle in his arms.

Wrapped in a towel was a great horned owl. He explained that he had hit the owl and was coming to me because he knew I loved animals and thought I might help. There was no wildlife clinic nearby, so we took the injured owl into our home that night. From our bookshelf, I retrieved a manual for treating injured wildlife.

At nearly two feet tall, great horned owls are one of the largest predatory birds in the ecosystem. Females are larger than the males. Their eyes are a haunting yellow, and their tufted ears are similar to those of a lynx. Their presence is intense.

That evening, we built a chicken-wire cage, placed the hissing, unhappy owl in it and moved it into a corner of our dining room. The next day, we drove to town and bought sulfa drugs, heavy-duty gloves, and liver so that we could feed the owl and set her broken wing. In the light of the kitchen window, I held her as Dean poured the sulfa drug into the wound on her wing; she shrieked in pain like a child. I had never been around a bird of prey; all three of us were frightened. We splinted and bandaged her wing as best we could, discovering that her beak and talons were like wire cutters. Despite the heavy-duty gloves, one nail pierced Dean's wrist.

We enlisted our neighbors and friends to collect dead mice for us, and we fed her liver rolled in eggshells as the wild animal care book recommended. The owl was wary of us. She either hissed like an angry cat or closed her eyes and looked away when we came near the cage. I was suspicious of her, too. She could hurt me with her sharp tools of beak and talon. She might strike at my daughters if they came too close. We walked around her cage with quiet care, moving slowly and gracefully as much to ease our anxieties as to show her we were not a threat.

Gradually, as the days darkened into winter over the next month or two, we became more at ease around one another, each of us less reactive to a potential threat. We began to share a reliable warmth of trust and to show gestures of love. She no longer hissed at us.

In time, she accepted food from our hands. We began to anticipate a ritual whenever we'd return to the cabin after a sojourn to town, work, or my mother's house. We would walk in the door and there would be the owl sitting proudly on the back of Dean's favorite chair.

Although her wounded wing prevented her from living in the wild again, once she had cut her way through the mesh of the cage, she could fly a short distance to the top of what became her favorite chair, too—the tallest one in the room facing the picture window.

Beyond the meadow was the woods. In the distance, one could see a bit of blue water. Honoring the owl, we let her sit for an hour or so on this perch to relish being queen of the cabin. Our daughters were age seven and five at the time, so we made sure they did not approach the owl too swiftly or closely; but she never did threaten them. We felt joy in her joy, and in seeing her feeling comfortable in her surroundings, claiming her place in the family. Then we would don the heavy-duty gloves, approach her from behind to grab her, put her back in the cage, and rewire it.

One day, as I slowly, soothingly moved my hand close to the cage, she allowed me to pet her head. As I touched her, she yielded and closed her eyes like a happy cat. After that, we were friends, family. I could stroke her astoundingly smooth-feathered head and the soft front of her breast. She felt fragile and small under her fluffy layer of feathers.

At night, she sang to other owls. From outside the window, we listened to the free owls calling back to her. Her resonant voice returned their song. Were they her family? Of course, she yearned for them. One of the saddest sounds one can hear is an owl calling out, unable to fly. I felt like an embarrassed eavesdropper on a private conversation I could not understand.

In the spring, we built a new cage outside for her, visible from the living room. By then, she had gradually gone blind. Milky cataracts covered her eyes. Owls are known to possess impeccably good vision and hearing. Outside in the cage, she could be closer to the other owls, the air, the trees—to her life before us.

One night, I dreamt I was walking out on a white dock over an inlet of the Salish Sea. The full moon hovered over the still waters. Moonlight formed a path of rippling glimmers out in front of the dock. The waters transformed into the palest lavender in the night. I stood quietly at the beginning of the pier, facing the sea. Overhead, I heard the whoosh of wings. Looking up, I saw a large white owl fly by, directly over the dock and into the distance, towards the West.

When I awoke that morning, I walked outside, as was my custom, to greet the owl. It was then that I saw her shrunken body lying in the cage, her spirit absent from it.

My daughters and I buried her ceremoniously under the tree we called the magic tree. This enormous, dark-green noble fir stands tall with symmetrical branches lifting towards the sky. We often visited this elegant evergreen to give praise and lift our hearts. Over the years, the owl's body has melded into the guardian tree.

After the owl passed, I confessed to a friend that I didn't think I had cared for her well enough.

"I've always felt guilty about not doing more for her," I shared.

My friend, a Harvard biologist, responded with factual yet consoling words: "When great horned owls are in captivity, they die within a week or so. They are never friendly and can never be tamed."

Relieved and surprised, I breathed in his words, and my heart settled. How fortunate I was to have had this owl for the time that I did. She was more than a guest or a friend; she was the teacher I had been seeking. Through her, I learned to carry the medicine of seeing through the dark. Her wise spirit remains with me and my family to this day.

Dr. Joanne Halverson

ANGST IS OPTIONAL

The steering wheel's thumb pads guide my hands, comfortably relaxed in the eight and four o'clock positions. I bounce in my seat as I drive along, the car radio pounding out a greatest-hits CD of songs from a popular punk/alternative rock band.

Today, the absent laughter of "Don't sing, Mom!" is underscored by soft snores. I smile into the rearview mirror at my middle-aged, black lab sprawled across the back seat. Her head rests in one of the booster seats, next to a partially completed Transformer toy. In the other, her back foot covers a Super Mario Brothers Game Boy game cartridge. My eyes look forward down the road once more, before I glance quickly at the front passenger seat. My tan-leather crossbody bag, the regular solo seat occupant, today shares the space with handwritten, pre-GPS directions. Mid-afternoon's yellow-orange warmth through the windshield, my favorite sunglasses, and well over halfway to an exciting new destination . . . I have always loved road trips.

But then, a wistfulness tightens across my face and I slowly stop bouncing. My heart reaches out toward my absent children. Rock music and dog snuffles fade from awareness, leaving only the underlying hum of the tires' white noise. This is the weekend my kiddos are not home, and by now I'd have thought that this could feel at least ordinary. Even after all this time, the lack of their presence is still alien. Incongruous. Painful, even. It feels wrong to travel without them, even though this particular excursion is planned.

Guilt. I adjust my hips side to side in my seat and lean forward, hands absently drifting back to my learned-and-outdated muscle memory of 10 and two on the wheel. My throat tightens. I swallow. Still thinking about my children, I consider why this particular trip is designed timing.

A few months ago, I'd met a person of interest and had been regularly connecting with him at a handful of his family gatherings here in the small town where I live. We'd also been talking daily on the phone in the evenings after the kids are asleep. This is our first time getting together, just the two of us, at his house two hours away . . . which means overnight.

What in the actual hell am I doing? Going to his house for the weekend? The weekend! As a first date! What kind of message does that send? What kind of woman am I? What kind of mother am I? I don't know this person, really. What am I getting myself into? I could turn around. I should turn around. I'm about half an hour away from my destination, an hour and a half back to the safety of home. I shouldn't be doing this. I can't do this. I don't do this.

Before I was married, I didn't date much, and I haven't discovered any joy in dating since it's been over. *I don't know how to do this. I can't do this.* I had thought that my intuition was guiding this, and now I'm super questioning it . . . and scared. *What if I got my intuition confused? What if what I thought had felt right is actually really wrong, again?*

I remove my sunglasses, wipe my forehead with the back of my hand and turn down the radio volume. I look around at the greening grass in the ditches, the burgeoning crops beyond, the sky with only a cloud or two gently leading me down the road. *What is happening to me?* My mind won't stop. I am losing control of my body. I am spiraling out of bounds, unusually and uncharacteristically.

I am hyperventilating now. Constricted left side of my chest, pounding. Blood in my ears, roaring. Tunnel vision. I have a vague notion that I need to focus on the road before it disappears from my awareness. *Do I pull over? I should pull over! Should I be driving in this escalating physical state? And what is this physical state, anyway? What in the world am I experiencing? How can this possibly be happening? I am being completely taken over by and separated from my body and this rising manic, mental loop of "I can't go . . . I can't do this . . . I can't . . . NO NO NO NO NO NO NO NO!"*

And then … appearing on the road ahead is a shadowy, wavelike motion. A medium-sized, dark mammal emerges into my lane from a wide ditch on the right. It crosses my path and moves into the vacant oncoming lane. This is not unusual, as various critter sightings are a regular part of my travels. This untamed, wild thing is far enough ahead that there is no danger of hitting it, yet close enough that I can't believe I haven't identified it so far. Involuntarily and completely captured by this mystery animal, my body and brain are arrested from their furious, uncontrolled frenzy. I am existing in one split second, yet synchronously frozen in extended time.

Leaning forward in wonder, my face scrunches in curious focus. *What is it?* Raccoon is an obvious choice, as it's quite common to see those permanently "sleeping" on the pavement around here. But this is the wrong shape and movement for a raccoon. *Could it be a skunk?* Nope, it's larger than that and it's wearing a uniformly colored, shiny coat. I see sleekness and a smooth gait. The movement is undulating. This creature is agile. It has a grace to its presence.

Just watching it in this moment, I feel my body begin to respond and relax. It feels like ripples, a lithe flow emanating through me. *What is it?* I take my foot off the gas pedal and coast closer to where this creature is safely crossing then dropping off into the ditch on the far side of the road. I am gliding now, releasing the pushing. Reshaping myself. Receiving. As I pass, the realization of what this creature is strikes me like lightning. It's an otter. Disbelief and reverence download into my being and I am fully halted from panic as I grip the wheel.

In my psyche, otter energy is imprinted as lighthearted, fun, encouragement to be more playful. Although I cross paths with many different animals on a regular day, I have rarely encountered otters. I glance around at both sides of the road, the mature oaks lining them, and the nearby farm fields of corn and sugar beets. *Otters live around water. Where is the water?*

This otter literally came out of nowhere: Now Here.

Still in a stupor of disbelief, I slow down to a near stop. The otter has safely crossed the road, presenting me with a clear view of itself the entire time. An otter for sure. Unmistakable.

My body is now flooded with an absolute and complete calm that does not at all match my frantic thinking. This is not coming from me. This is an external feeling from someone or something else. I am not the source of this feeling. It is being bestowed upon me. My mind is still spinning yet my body and spirit are calm. I feel slightly disoriented, aware yet unafraid. This awareness is also being given to me in this moment. This is how I know it's not of myself. And then, my mind catches up and matches my body and spirit, and it calms. It can't not. I feel only peace. Holy wow. Open-mouthed, I collapse back into my seat in astonishment as I glide forward, the otter vanishing into the dry ditch as I slide by.

On the heels of this peace, I explode into a feeling of happiness and ecstasy. This feeling is a gift. I am full-bodied joyous! I am being shown, through feeling, what otter represents to me, and the meaning is that there is no need for panic. Worry not about this weekend, and all that it entails. I am in tune with my intuition, and following Divine guidance. I don't doubt this now. I am being encouraged to lighten up, to find the fun in the unknowns of this very situation, in this exact moment, with this specific person. To enjoy. It is safe for me to do so. In fact, it is part of a bigger plan for me to do so. Although I won't fully realize it until many years later, this is a pivotal point in the timeline of my life.

Spirit is showing me through otter energy that this path not only is nothing to fear, but also has the potential for incredible, deep, lifelong joy down this road. *I am safe. This is right. Go see this person. For the entire weekend. My fears are unfounded. He is not going to turn out to be a serial killer, or a narcissist, or yet again a master manipulator. He's not even going to turn out to be a waste of time. He is truly a good soul. This is a gift.*

What's more, I'm being shown why I was heading in this spiraling direction of uncharacteristic panic in the first place. Spirit is encouraging me to do the very thing I doubted: To trust. To take a leap of heart and faith. To see what unfolds from here. Not only is this situation okay, it is necessary. It is Divine guiding, Divine timing.

I swallow my fear, which now magically tastes like trust and surrender. In these moments, I am transformed. My face cannot stop smiling. My body is vibrating. I am exuberance. I am expansive. I am light. I am euphoria. I am rapture. This is not my plan, but Spirit's. Surrender, and follow this.

I throw back my head and look up through the open sunroof at the blue sky dotted with sparse, puffy clouds. And I surge forward—foot pressing down on the gas pedal, elbows straight and strong—joy erupting from every cell.

Then I hear laughter. Oh wait, that's me.

Gina Drellack

THANK YOU, TICK

was raised to have an appreciation for all animals. My mom used to bring injured animals to the veterinarian. My stepdad would charm stray cats until they adopted us as their owners. My uncle occasionally pulled over on the side of the road to escort birds and amphibians to safety. We would play in the yard and observe spiders, bees, and the occasional field mouse close up; but truth be told, I had a fear and loathing for ticks.

As the mother of a baby, a toddler, and a preschooler, I am aware that deer ticks can be carriers of Lyme's Disease, so I take precautions to protect my children. One day, I was at home with my children enjoying our daily tea party, or what others might call lunch. We'd brought everything out to a blanket on the front lawn—sandwiches, sippy cups, fruit slices, and other snacks. It was a beautiful sunny day, but at one point, a cloud moved in front of the sun, prompting me to take off my sunglasses.

When I did so, my eyes followed a carrot stick that my toddler had just thrown across the blanket. I picked it up, but my eyes lingered. There was a movement just beyond the snack basket. I looked closer.

Right there on a blade of grass near the blanket was a tiny tick . . . a deer tick. Clear as day, I watched it walk across the blade of grass and onto the blanket.

"Okay!" I said hastily. "That was a fun tea party. Now we're going inside for tick checks! Come, babies, let's work together to get everything inside."

We gathered everything up and shuffled across to the back of the house and into the bathroom, which has excellent lighting to illuminate any freckle that might be an insect. When we emerged from the bathroom, tick free, I felt relieved and ready to take the children back outside, maybe for some chalk drawing, bubble blowing, or water painting.

Then I noticed something unusual out the front window. I walked towards it and saw that a neighbor's tree had fallen. Did it rain while we were in the bathroom? There was no thunder or lightning. What had happened?

Walking outside, I realized that a massive tree trunk had split and fallen across our driveway. I stood in quiet shock as I spotted the huge broken branches strewn across where we'd had our tea party just moments earlier. A live electrical line was down in the front yard, as well.

Wow. I let that sink in. Had we still been outside playing and eating lunch, the children would have been traumatized and possibly even badly injured by the fallen tree or power line.

It crossed my mind: *Did that tick know something I didn't know? Is it possible that it showed up to help us, not hurt us?*

The next day, I learned on the news that the damage was caused by a microburst that was being investigated as a possible tornado. As I listened to the weather segment, I was overwhelmed with gratitude for that little tick that was clearly sent to us as a Divine messenger. Its presence was the only thing that could have urged me to move my children into the house that quickly.

Thank you, Tick.

Misa Myers

OWL MUSE

*I*t was a warm, clear evening and I decided to enjoy dinner on the deck, surrounded by the red and yellow hues of autumn leaves on the trees. No sooner had I swallowed the first bite when . . . whoosh! . . . a huge barred owl swooped out of nowhere, landing on a bird feeder hooked onto the corner of the deck.

Startled by its grand entrance, I stared in amazement at this enchanted creature looking over its shoulder at me with impossibly huge eyes. My rational brain went crazy: *Doesn't she know my two cats, Sirius and Libby, are on the deck? Why would she land in a clearly lit space when owls prefer the dark? What would cause her to land here, eight feet away, and why now?*

I knew that magic was afoot. I took in every inch of her beautiful, banded, brown-and-white stripes and round marble eyes, imprinting the moment on my heart. I knew she had come for a reason. The synchronicity of the timing was too great! That day, I had started writing my first book . . . and now an owl practically drops in my lap?

I wanted to call for my husband but knew it would break the spell. Mesmerized, I watched as the owl's eyes deliberately traversed from Sirius to

Libby to me. She held my gaze for several seconds and I felt a hundred gigabytes of her owl medicine transmit into my being. Then, as silently as she had landed, her feathered body whispered away.

Various feelings ran through me at once: Stunned. Honored. Incredulous. Elated. Buzzing. I stumbled into the house to tell my husband, but my words came out in barely intelligible fits and starts: "honey . . . owl . . . oh my God . . . you missed . . . unbelievable . . . my book . . . did you see it?"

The next day, my body was still electric from the experience. I went online to research the type of owl I'd just seen. I finally found two suitable images, which I printed, laminated, and ceremonially placed in a prominent position on my bulletin board. They occupied that spot for over a year.

This barred owl became my muse as I worked on my manuscript. From her vantage point above my desk, she watched over my process. I felt her soft, wise presence daily, and sensed that my book was being infused with sweet medicine.

I knew that owls have strong mythical associations in many indigenous cultures. In reading through various references and listening to my own heart, I recognized that she came to imbue me with multiple layers of wisdom. She was there to help me drop even more deeply into my feminine intuition, receptivity, and connection to the unseen realms. It was an essential link, as I invoked my spiritual team and the Great Mystery every time I sat down to write.

The owl shared her gifts with me in other subtler ways, as well, including mentorship in the use of my voice. Most of all, I was grateful for her steadfast companionship and ability to hold loving, continuous space for this massive undertaking of writing a book.

As the coming few years came and went, so did a variety of milestones: the day I completed writing the book, the day it was accepted for publication, the day it was printed. I wondered if I would see an owl again to commemorate these achievements.

In the week leading up to the launch date, however, I developed a terrible sinus infection that took me out for the better part of a month. I was frustrated at the timing, worried that I still had so much to do to get ready. I'm sure my system just couldn't bear the intense pace I had been operating at for a number of months. My body was forcing me to slow down, recover, and have faith that everything was as it should be, and that I had done what I needed to do. It was another opportunity to trust that I unenthusiastically accepted.

Finally, launch day arrived, a momentous occasion for any first-time author. I knew this day represented the completion of several major initiatory cycles, both personally and professionally. These initiations also signified that I had reached a new level of adeptness and trust in my relationship with my spirit guides (who heavily influenced the manuscript), as well as preparation to leap onto a larger public stage. It was clear that I was being called to step into much bigger shoes than I had ever walked in before.

I reflected on all that it took to get me to that point. I was grateful, proud, expectant, excited, drained, and fulfilled. I moved through the day with an eager and well-earned exhaustion.

When falling asleep that night, suspended in that liminal space between consciousness and the ethers, the magic materialized once more. I heard the *hoot! hoot! hoot!* of a great horned owl. She had come!

I leapt from the bed to see if I could spot the owl against the dark sky on a nearby rooftop or utility pole. I did not see her, but I heard her once again. Then I happened to catch the time on the clock. It was 10:17.

A few groggy seconds later, I cocked my head like a curious dog. *What was the date I had begun writing my book? Could it be true? Was it possible?* I flipped back through my calendar and there, on October 17, were my notes "start book" and "owl."

October 17, or 10:17.

As the final gate of this three-year initiatory cycle closed, my sweet owl muse came to bracket the portal and herald the birth of my book. The journey was complete. I had passed the initiation. My baby (book) had fledged, left the nest, and now had a life of her own. I fell asleep with a deep sense of peace.

Rev. Stephanie Red Feather, Ph.D.

MAGPIE

*a*n Australian magpie swooped down from the Queensland gum tree that towers above my deck and perched on the railing directly facing me. I had been living in my suburban Melbourne house for eight years and knew that magpies can be curious and territorial birds.

By then, the magpies and I had an unspoken agreement: The garden is their space and the deck is mine. They typically stay in the trees that overlook it.

That day, one magpie overrode the house rules. I was sitting on the cedar boards of my deck as I often do on pleasant afternoons. The late spring sun warmed my body and felt comforting to my soul after coming out of a long, challenging Covid-19 lockdown. Those months had me spending more time outdoors than ever before.

The magpie landed just a few inches away and looked me straight in the eye. I felt as if she had been watching me from the tree and was making a point to get my attention. I stared back in surprise and wonder, having never come so close to one of these birds. Her soft grey-and-white coloring signified that she was a younger female. Her energy was softer and less aggressive than some of the others.

As she blinked at me with her shiny black eyes, I felt a frequency shift. She had medicine. I could feel it. Then she hopped down to the deck floor and casually stood a few inches from my knee, still not taking her eyes off of me.

"Why are you here, magpie?" I asked in a whisper so as to not scare her away.

She peered at me for nearly a minute, her movements slight. I felt the subtlest sensation like something invisible was penetrating my energy field through her stare. I instinctively knew that she was offering me something. It was soft and faint—a sort of energetic gift that was yet to be unwrapped. Then she broke her focus and flew off.

"I want to know why I'm here and where I'm going," a client asked me in one of our sessions three days prior. "I'm ready to know now. Can you help me understand my purpose?"

As a spiritual practitioner, I've been asked this question many times by many clients. I help them answer it by connecting in and channeling through information on their behalf. I typically see a lot in these sessions. It's like my spirit soars above the trees and I can see all vantage points clearly.

After this session three days earlier, my client's question weighed heavily on me. For the truth is, I seemed to be able to see everyone else's path and direction but my own. Increasingly, I was becoming *not* okay with that. Where I saw long, beautiful winding paths for others, I had been seeing only a big wall in front of mine.

When I felt into what lies beyond that wall, I'd get a sense of unease in the pit of my stomach—not because what was coming was bad or traumatic, but because it made me uncomfortable in ways that I knew all too well. It was the same discomfort I'd usually feel when promoting my work by going live on social media or posting a video for the world to view. It was a fear of being publicly seen.

Two days later, one of my best friends wanted to talk with me about his future. He, too, was questioning his decisions and his life's path. My fears around my own future resurfaced with even greater heaviness.

I'm ready to let these fears go and truly know my path, I said to myself.

An hour later, she showed up on the deck railing . . . the magpie.

When the night's stillness had settled in and the magpies had stopped their warbling and gone to sleep, I downloaded an eBook by a First Nations author. As I nestled in to read it, cedar oil from my diffuser filling the air, I was taken back to Canada, my birth country . . . back to when the magic of medicine began. Since I have a dash of Mi'kmaq and Metis in my bloodlines, the stories from my native land gently called me back home.

My crown started to buzz after reading the first story, like little fireworks exploding above my head. This is always a sign that the Spirit world wants to talk to me. I opened to the energy and invited it in.

Magpie immediately came to my attention. A vision of my encounter with her hours earlier flashed through my mind—her energy flying around my field with expectation. The gravity I had been feeling around my path grew denser, as though it was time to see my future.

But that wall . . . it's big . . . and it's scary on the other side. I don't want to be seen, recognized, burned at the witch stake . . . because underneath the outer parts of me that the world sees is a deeply spiritual person who is trying to live within the safe confines of my spiritual closet. It's a comfy closet. I've lived here a long time.

Magpie's medicine intensified even more. She showed me my fear of being seen and turned me around to look at it.

Face it. Don't be afraid of it, she communicated.

I shifted in my seat, suddenly deeply uncomfortable in my comfortable chair. She showed me the truth—that what I was feeling was an old story from another time and place, carried through the fabric of space to the here and now.

You are here to be on camera for anyone in the world to see.

"I'm not okay with that," I respond rather bluntly.

She sent me a vision to both mock my fear and calm me from it: I'm sitting in my office in front of my computer, camera lights on. Client after client is watching me channel through Zoom. I am speaking to groups of people from every continent except Antarctica. In this future vision, I've been living this and doing this for six years.

As my energy calms, I'm not sure if the wall was dissolving along with my fears or if I was rising up above it . . . but I started to see the truth . . . and it set me free.

There it was—the path forward. I couldn't make out much detail but for the first time, I wasn't afraid to visibly walk it. I wasn't so afraid of who saw me.

Magpie came back a few days later, shortly after I had finished a client session and was still in a semi-expanded state of consciousness. She didn't look at me directly. Instead, she cocked her head sideways as if to study me from all angles, shifting her head in little curious jerks, as if scanning my energy. I had the feeling that she was about to speak to me telepathically with a final message that I needed to hear . . . and I wanted to receive it.

So, I grabbed my writing journal and tuned in. The words landed softly in my being:

Have you gotten the message yet? Your fears are just that . . . fears. They slow you down. They've caused you to walk backwards and carefully tiptoe toward your future, afraid to embrace the gift of your presence and what you are here to bring forth. It's time to dream bigger and embrace who you are. I've brought healing. Please accept. I'll be back again to see you.

Magpie returned a few more times over the coming months, landing on the cedar boards not far from where I was sitting. As promised, she was just checking in on me, micro dosing me with more of her medicine with each encounter. Those visits dismantled the remaining remnants of the wall to my future and my fears associated with it . . . until all that remained was a bright, sunny path ahead.

These days, I sometimes see magpie out in the garden with her mate searching for grubs and other edibles. She barely acknowledges me as I call out to her. Her medicine is done.

Yolanda Tong

OVERCOMING FEAR WITH HELP FROM THE WHALES

*S*even of us are floating on a tiny, inflatable watercraft in the deep, cold waters of Clayoquot Sound in the Pacific Ocean, just off Canada's West Coast. I'm outfitted in a flotation suit—a head-to-toe, long-sleeved, orange garment that retains body heat and assures buoyancy, should we capsize. Knowing this helps calm my nerves as we set out for our sea faring adventure. I'm exhilarated and terrified at the same time. *How did I get here?*

Months prior, the idea of a whale-watching trip had been an exciting theory while it was under discussion amongst my husband Arne and I, and our close friends, Tracy and Stuart. Our plans for a camping trip to the village of Tofino on Vancouver Island had always included an excursion to see killer whales, humpback whales, or gray whales—some of the largest animals on earth.

Once in Tofino, however, I'm scared at just the thought of setting foot on this 19-foot, rubber Zodiac boat, let alone venturing in a huge body of water in a remote part of the world to potentially encounter gigantic marine animals. I actually dread being around these huge creatures, feeling literally afraid for my life . . . and the idea of capsizing in the frigid Pacific waters is very real to me.

The morning of our planned excursion, I had shared my fears with our friends. Tracy didn't shame me or try to take my emotions away. She offered to stay on land with me while Arne and Stuart go looking for whales. My shoulders relaxed and I could breathe again.

"Let's go and have tea at the Wickaninnish Inn overlooking Chesterman's Beach while the guys are whale watching," Tracy suggested.

I imagined myself warm and cozy in the tea house, perched between the ancient rainforest and the sea, with a view of the rugged natural beauty of British Columbia, amid thousand-year-old forests of spruce, hemlock, and western cedar. It sounded delightful.

With our day rearranged, Tracy and I went with Arne and Stuart to drop them off at the pier before we headed to the inn for tea. Once at The Whale Centre, we meandered in to look around. The guys were putting on their flotation suits and I figured I may as well try one on. That way, I could experience wearing a survival suit without going on the boat.

Once in the suit, I realized that I'd gotten this far. In the spirit of adventure, I changed my mind and decided to join in the whale watching trip. After the four of us suited up, we descended from the wooden dock with another couple who would be accompanying us and hopped into the wobbly Zodiac, along with a driver/guide.

So here I am, ready to venture into the moody indigo waters. The small engine hums, sputters, and comes alive. The resilient coastline of wind-swept bright green fir trees coming right down to the water's edge recedes and the expanse of ocean increases. The boat is so low to the water that I can reach my hand down and touch its liquid coolness. The only sound is the boat's little outboard engine.

We travel a way, and time becomes endless. We see a few killer whale fins slicing through the water in the distance through the low-hanging fog. Then the guide turns off the engine and there is ethereal silence, a wide stretch of stillness that goes on and on. Full and penetrating quiet. We bob on the water, feeling tranquil, satisfied, each one of us in our individual zones of inner connection to the natural world. We don't need idle conversation. We're in a place of reverence and contentment.

A "whoosh" sound suddenly breaks the silence as a gray whale blows and surfaces for air. The tip of its head comes out of the water followed by the large oval blowhole right on top of its head. I am about seven feet away from the whale. As it swims under our boat, the whale knows precisely where it is in relation to our vessel. The blowhole opens for the whale to exhale, then it inhales and closes the hole using its large muscles before it dives.

The mottled, black-and-creamy-white blowhole is at least the size of a basketball. I smell the briny scent of wild fish from the resting water on top of the whale's nostrils. My face is wet from the light mist of the whale's exhaled breath. The moisture is heavy enough to coat my eyelids and drip down my face.

The water is so clear and the whale so close that I can inspect the spots and smears of color on its body. The whale's exhalation washes all fear fully out of me. There is no trace of scare or worry or apprehension. I am in a place of complete trust, complete and utter safety. A sensation of protection and security comes over me like I have never felt before. Time stands still. I am in the presence of greatness, yet greatness without ego, without fanfare, without pomp and circumstance.

The giant mammal's salty breath blesses me. I am baptized by the whale. As it dives deeper and swims away, I hear it speak to me in a way I have not experienced before. I don't hear the words through my ears, or through the air from the whale to me. I hear and sense its low-clear words resonating in the middle of my brain—an inner hearing, with my body, heart, and spirit, yet truly physical.

The whale's voice comes from within its own depth of being as it enters me and says, *We are the ancient ones. We are the ancient ones.*

Adair Wilson Heitmann

AN ADAMANT VOICE TO HEAL THE HORSE

*L*ate one Thursday night about 20 years ago, while writing in my home office in Coarsegold, California, I received a call from my office manager, Lindy, that would ultimately change the course of my spiritual work and life. There was a notable sadness in her voice as she asked to have off that Friday morning.

Lindy owns a small horse ranch in the golden California hills of the Sierra Nevada Mountains, where she keeps five show horses safe and well fed. She is a devoted professional Western Pleasure Show rider. That morning on the call, Lindy explained that she had to take her favorite show horse to the veterinarian to have her put down. The horse couldn't eat or drink and was very sick and close to dying. I concurred without hesitation.

No sooner had I put the phone down when I heard a towering voice over my left side, about three feet above my head saying, *Heal the horse!*

Whoa! Did I just hear God speaking? I knew someone or something was on the other side of that voice.

Besides being stunned, I got quite nervous. My body felt a jolt and everything became silent. *Heal the horse? Me?* I continued with my writings but couldn't help ponder what had just happened. The voice was too loud to be my intuition. Where did it come from?

A few minutes later, again, the voice repeated: *Heal the horse!*

Hmmm. This time, the tone was adamant. My mind raced and every cell in my body seemed to echo.

I don't like horses! I responded in my mind.

I had a reason for feeling this way. Years ago, as a young adult, I lived in New York City. I was a true city slicker and not an animal lover in the least. One weekend, I went with a few friends to Pennsylvania on a nature outing and we decided to go horseback riding. I remembered being scared as a child just riding a donkey in the park! I truly feared riding a horse, but on that trip with friends, I decided to give it a try, thinking that I could conquer this lifelong fear. What I didn't know then is that horses are extremely sensitive to humans' emotions.

Well, I wasn't long into the trails when my horse decided he didn't want me riding him anymore. He tried to warn me by nipping hard on my leg. We calmed him down but after a few more minutes, he reared on his hind legs and screeched in an effort to throw me off his back.

With those memories still harbored in my mind, I wondered, *How in the heck can I heal a horse?*

Nonetheless, I felt empathy for Lindy and wanted to help if I could. I called my friend Terry, an animal intuitive, and asked if she'd go to the ranch with me the following day. Terry agreed. I called Lindy to let her know that we'd be there around eight o'clock.

That morning, Terry and I drove through the beautiful redwood forest on the way to the ranch. Lindy greeted us with coffee and homemade doughnuts as we sat on the front porch discussing the situation. Then she gave us a quick tour of the ranch, ending up in the stables.

Lindy slowly walked the ailing horse out from her stable, a beautiful palomino with striking color contrasts. We walked around the horse a few times, chatting about the logistics of the healing session. All the while, I kept hearing, *Heal the horse*, over and over.

For the first time in decades—possibly in my life—I began to experience compassion for a horse. I wanted to help her. My mind started to focus on giving the palomino new energies of life. After circling her a few times more, I stopped, sincerely prayed, and asked the Holy Spirit for guidance on what to do.

From there, Spirit orchestrated the event, with each of us doing our part. My heart opened wide as I embraced the palomino and looked into her eyes. Terry held her head and using reiki and other protocols, we started to move energy to ground the horse. Lindy had invited a local student acupuncturist to help, as well. She placed her needles around the lower abdominal region of the horse while Terry and I worked at her head and feet. Those moments felt truly inspired by the Divine, as if we'd all been summoned—Lindy, Terry, me, the student, the palomino, the ranch, even the trees along the drive to the ranch. Each of us experienced a consequence from this precious encounter.

Within 20 minutes or so, Terry signaled for me to come to the front of the horse where she was standing.

"Robert, look at this," she said, pointing to the palomino's eyes. I noticed tears rolling down her face. My heart dropped, not realizing that an animal could cry like this.

Terry and I kept moving and grounding the horse's energy for the next 15 minutes or so. Slowly, she began to lift her head, as if gaining strength and composure. She even passed gas a few times. Soon she was meandering about and taking sips of water. Lindy placed a feed bag on the palomino's snout, and she started to nibble on the feed.

Within an hour or so, we all had smiles on our faces. Something big had shifted. As Terry and I got ready to leave, we took one last look at the palomino, who was now gaiting around the corral.

Later that evening, Lindy called to say that she had taken the horse to the veterinarian, who was quite astonished upon hearing the news of what had transpired that morning.

Today, Lindy's palomino is still healthy and well—in fact, she delivered a beautiful foal.

This experience altered something significant in me beyond alleviating my fear of horses. My recurrent pet allergies and itchiness virtually disappeared, as well, but most importantly, my perception and compassion for all animals substantially increased. The laws of the universe had worked a beautiful magic on me. Both the horse and I were healed that day, our lives forever changed.

Robert V. Gerard

TIME TO TRUST

*a*long trot a few horses into the grassy, sun-dappled field at Remus, an equine sanctuary set in the green rolling hills of Essex, England.

One of them, named Dolly, grips my attention. I ask Dolly if she wants me to approach her. She physically nods *yes*. Dolly lifts her left leg several times, prompting me to ask:

"Would you like me to help you with your leg?"

Again, Dolly nods four times as if to playfully say, *Yes, come on and get your arse over here already!*

As I stand at her side with my hand over an old scar on her left leg, Dolly's soft, brown hair shimmers in the sunlight. When I finish and thank her for sharing reiki, she bows her head.

It's a short interaction but these moments with Dolly have a profound impact on me. She is teaching me to trust my communication skills with animals and trust myself in all matter of ways, as well.

I've always loved animals and being in their presence fills my soul with light. Ever since my older sister brought our neighbor's velvety, black-haired kitten, Elvis, into our home for a visit when I was four years old, I've known that animals are sentient beings. Even saying hello to the cows and sheep in the fields of Somerset in the UK where I grew up always gave me a sense of fulfilment.

Yet over the decades, I couldn't hear my soul calling. I realized at some point that I had not been trusting myself and sensed that the animals would bring me back to my soul connection. About five years ago, I learned about animal reiki and was immediately drawn in by it. I wanted to feel worthy of living with the magic of animals and trust in my ability to help both animals and people. I decided to pursue reiki training, which led me to that weekend workshop at Remus.

The sanctuary has large stables and rusty outbuildings that are home to Shetland ponies, donkeys, sheep, goats, cows, a half dozen cats, and a dog. After sharing delightful tea and biscuits on our first morning together, the other workshop participants and I were off to the stables to be with the horses. Each of us had an opportunity to enter one of the pastures where numerous horses were grazing—which is where I first encountered Dolly. Once in the fields, we had time to privately meditate and take in the equine energy.

After working with Dolly, the second horse that I interacted with that day also helped me recognize that it is safe to trust in the healing energy I'm working with. Minstral is a wonderful girl with extraordinary markings around her face that remind me of Egyptian hieroglyphs. As I practiced reiki near Minstral, she stopped her busy grazing, raised her head, and slung her face over the stable door to hang out in the healing energy. She got as close as she could to me and my workshop partner, and stayed there for the entire session, giving us confirmation that it felt good. After the session, a gentle nudge of empowerment from Minstral seemed to communicate, *Samantha, you've got this.*

Next it was time to work with the donkeys at the sanctuary. I walked slowly to the gate where these precious animals were all quite happily scoffing their food out in the green, lush pasture. As I got comfortable and started my meditation, the entire pack (bar one) walked up to me and stood close. I held the space for about 15 minutes, with a few sighs and a couple tongues hanging out—theirs, not mine—all relaxed and relishing this sacred space.

When I went to leave, one of the larger donkeys put his head over the gate. We touched for 30 seconds or so while I silently said *thank you*. Then the rest of the smaller donkeys lined up in a queue—head to tail—to thank me all at once. I couldn't believe what I was witnessing. The communication was so clear.

After spending 30 seconds with each donkey, the last one in line stayed with me—first placing his head in my hands, then moving slowly and gently against the gate with my hands on him. He stopped when I placed my hands on his hips and we stayed there for another 10 minutes. Finally, I stepped away and when I turned back, he gently put his head in my hands once more. We said our mutual *thank you's* and off he trotted to join the others. It was magical. The donkeys further reinforced that I can trust in myself and that I don't need to try so hard to connect with the animals. I just need to be me. I am enough.

I completed the retreat at Remus feeling more certain than ever that animals hold such wisdom if we are open to listening to it. They continue to teach me to not give up, to be inquisitive, chill out, have fun and play, and just be present.

Samantha Roe

RIGHT WHERE I'M SUPPOSED TO BE

You must go. This is the message Spirit gave me when offered an opportunity to do a sound bath at a retreat being hosted by an acquaintance I'd met in Sedona.

"Heck yes!" I said, excited to "do my thing" and be of service.

Things got awkward, however, as the logistics of the retreat were planned. The details shifted from my running the two days to being told I had to pay to be there. I didn't feel I was supposed to run the event, but I wanted to be honored for my contribution. In the past, I had lost important things because I didn't speak up for myself. I was afraid of being judged and, in this case, losing the great friendship I had formed with the person hosting the retreat.

I was ready to jump ship. That's when Spirit stepped in and said that I must still go. I grabbed my courage, took a risk to honor my guidance, and initiated another conversation with the host.

"Would you prefer to just come to the retreat and be paid for your sound bath?" she asked.

While the fee being offered was barely worth the commitment of eight to 10 hours, the packing, the drive, the setup of all my instruments, and to lead the practice, I said yes.

As I drove to the retreat that day, feeling shaky, I kept confirming with Spirit: *Are you sure? Am I crazy? Am I worthy?* Along the drive, I kept seeing hawks everywhere! It was like they were leading me there and building up my courage.

You are listening accurately, they seemed to say. *You are going the right way and doing the right thing.*

By the time I arrived, I felt confident and ready to serve. I thanked the hawks for the affirmation and ventured in to set up for the sound bath. We were in a magnificent space with a huge wall of windows overlooking the valley.

When the group arrived, I began my talk. Right in the middle of my pre-chat, a woman in the audience blurted out:

"Stacy! Stacy!"

"Yes?" I replied, slightly shocked that she was interrupting me.

"Look!" She pointed towards the window.

What I saw when I turned around nearly brought me to my knees and to tears. Flying right outside the window were . . . not one, not two . . . but four magnificent hawks, gliding through the air in figure-eight style, giving everyone a show.

Their message was clear: *We're here. We're supporting you.*

"What does that mean?" the woman asked.

"It means that I am right where I am supposed to be."

That day, the hawks gave me a great gift. Now, I do my best to honor my "knowing and no'ing" instead of my need to please others. Thank you, Hawk Spirit, for a day I will never forget.

Stacy Corley ≈ A.P.

A CROW ON MY HEAD

feel scared, hyped, panicked . . . but, strangely, fully alive. *What is happening?* A man honks his horn and rolls down his window as I'm walking down the sidewalk.

"Is that a *crow* on your head?" he asks, laughing hysterically.

I take off running down the street . . . *whoosh! whoosh!* . . . and the crow follows me, flying right above my head.

You can't ditch me that easily! he communicates.

Rounding the corner to my downtown apartment, I finally manage to dodge the crow. I take a moment to come back into my body and breathe deeply as the reality of what just happened begins to land. It's eight o'clock on a cool, foggy Tuesday morning and I had just finished teaching a flow yoga class at my downtown studio. *Did I call in that crow somehow?* My mind wants to analyze this but I am aware enough to know that this is beyond an ordinary experience.

Upon returning home, I am immediately guided to research the shamanic meaning of crow. What I learn doesn't surprise me—so many wonderful spiritual meanings! This further leads me to research dreamwork to better understand the dreams I'd been having since I was a child. With this nudge to do dreamwork, I sense that Mr. Crow is already beginning to shift my experience for the better.

The day of that initial encounter on the street, crow opened a portal to another world. For the next few days, while walking through town to my studio, I avoided going near what I now call "crow corner", the place where he first found me. I admit, I was scared yet curious. I would look for him but stay on the other side of the street—even donning a hat and sunglasses so I would fade into the street traffic.

Much to my dismay, it didn't work. About a week later, as I was walking to teach yoga, I heard that *whoosh! whoosh!* again and saw him coming at me. I started to run then BAM! He's on my head! Oh my! Oddly, I felt exhilarated to be reunited with him. *It doesn't matter what I wear or where I walk . . . there is no escaping Spirit, is there?* I think.

With that encounter, he gifted me with the guidance to use crow tarot. I purchased cards that now serve as my personal deck. The guidance that it gives me is impeccable. It never ceases to amaze me how spot-on the messages are.

After a year of integrating my dreams, working with signs and symbols in the tarot, and listening more sensitively to the crows in my neighborhood, I decide that I want to formally befriend a crow. So, I try to tune into the crows that perch on a wire in front of my apartment around late afternoon every day, I'm not successful.

One morning, I show up to teach high school on my campus a few miles from town. It's foggy, crisp, and very quiet. I arrive before anyone else is on campus .. . and out jumps Mr. Crow! He dive-bombs off the ceiling in the hallway, buzzes right by me then flies out the window and into a field. Whoa! I run to the window and watch him circle the basketball court then return to his perch across the street.

From that day forward, he continues to watch me. *I do have a crow friend!*

This was the beginning of the relationship I had been asking for. We have gotten to know each other. I named him Joe. I make it a point to bring peanuts to work and place them in the same spot every morning before the students come in. I use a particular sound at the back of my throat to inform him when I have arrived.

He comes when I "caw", flying close to me then respectfully waiting until I enter the classroom before he eats his treats. Crow is teaching me to be consistent because I have to remind myself to use the same sound, put the food in the same place, and say hello each day before I go to class. Using intention when interacting with him is grounding for me. It helps me to let go of my overactive brain and intense desire to multitask.

The spiritual seeker in me wonders, *Does Spirit simply find us? Pick us up? Bring us surprises that we never could see coming?* That part of me needs to know the answers.

My spirit tells me that through these encounters, I have found a desire to get comfortable with the uncomfortable, and to get out of my head.

I singled you out because you are happy and full of delight, my crow friend Joe has communicated to me. *Be kind to me and you will learn to be kind to yourself. I can see from up here that you aren't lost; you just think you are at times. You're on the right track. It's okay to let go and breathe because I've got your back.*

Lisa Marie Byars

THE CHARISMA CONNECTION

From the moment the breeder let Charisma loose in the arena, there was no denying her talent and powerful spirit. The two-year-old Morgan mare effortlessly trotted with her knees up to her chin, hocks digging into the earth, dirt flying, head held high. An undeniable presence, Charisma embodied the essence of her name. I knew she was the one . . . my next show horse.

Little did I know that this beautiful animal was going to be—in an act of self-preservation—the most important purchase of my life. I was at a low point. Two years earlier, I had lost my sister to suicide. She was my lifelong horse partner. Our equine passion intimately bonded us, as if we shared a soul around our love of these animals.

Time had passed yet my grief was still palpable as I tried to make sense of how she could take her life. My sister had struggled with depression since childhood, but I always thought her love of horses would save her . . . and now I was finding myself in that same spot. With depression and survivor's guilt, I felt little joy in any of the things that once filled me—even the horses.

Now, I was going to have Charisma. As her previous owner and I worked out the details, I felt excitement mixed with a mild apprehension. It was the first horse that I had chosen without the advice of counsel. I just jumped in and trusted my inner compass.

That evening, I awoke in the middle of a dream. A little disorientated, I looked at the clock and realized that only an hour had passed since I shut my eyes. Lying in bed, every cell in my body tingled. The dream was so vivid that it seemed more real than my waking state.

In it, I was with Charisma. All of her energy centers were open, as were mine. My body was being activated by the energetic connection between the two of us as shafts of light from her chakras connected with mine.

I didn't know what to do with this experience. I had just started to learn about the chakras and energy medicine. Intuitively, I knew it was somehow connected to my sister. Could her energy be in this horse? Does that kind of thing happen?

I didn't get much time to immerse myself in my human plans of having Charisma in the show ring. Ten days after I purchased her, Charisma fractured a piece of cartilage in her left hind leg. She was diagnosed with a congenital condition that could be career-ending. With so much angst and emotion to wade through, I needed to decide whether to send her for surgery or back to the breeder.

Distraught and confused, I felt as if the rug had been pulled out from under my feet. My veterinarian highly suggested sending Charisma back to the breeder, but something deep inside was prompting me to keep her. I spent a day or two in conflict between the voice of my head and the voice of my heart. But that dream! Wasn't it a message from Spirit?

A few days later, we took Charisma to Cornell University to have bilateral hock surgery. My heart won the first of many internal arguments to follow when I was forced to shift my focus from training Charisma to healing her.

Thank God I owned a barn and it was summer because this type of injury takes a minimum of three months of stall rest, with daily wrapping, cold water hosing, and hand walking the horse. Keeping all four hooves on the ground was a challenge for me and a young horse. We used that time to get to know each other's personalities and develop a bond without an agenda—a foundational piece that I had never really paid much attention to with my previous horses.

Living with horses had already increased my ability to feel into these animals, but those early days with Charisma were like flying in the dark. My emotional body was starting to come alive. I was beginning to sense energy and emotion but didn't know what to do with the information. This all spurred me to ask deeper questions.

Were horses more aware than I had been taught? What about that crazy dream? Do horses have souls? Did God have a hand in leading me to Charisma? Does our energy influence our horses? Did her leg condition have something to do with me since I had an injury to the same part of my body—the result of a nasty fall from a horse? Is there a better way to train horses than what I knew? Do horses show up to heal us? Could horses help us to connect to ourselves and ultimately the Divine?

I felt so alone on this journey, and my family thought I was going off the deep end in my quest to understand more about the interconnectedness of life.

Charisma's leg healed amazingly well, and our show ring career started two years later when she was four years old. She was off-the-charts talented and loved being in the limelight. Everyone would gather around the rail at the end of a class just to watch Charisma and me do a victory pass. I had quite a few offers from others wanting to purchase her. The thought hadn't entered my mind. I was feeling my passion again and I, too, loved the show ring.

Once Charisma was out of her junior horse years, I expected more out of her in order to compete with the professional trainers. Surprisingly, I found myself having challenging moments with her. Moments turned into days, weeks, and quite a few show seasons. There I was in the show ring asking to be judged, and now I found myself beginning to harshly judge myself and doubt my abilities.

Harnessing Charisma's power continued to test me. My techniques and training tools were not enough. We won many blue ribbons but our rides included anxiety and timing issues, which added up to small technical mistakes. The seamless performance I desired wasn't there, and I certainly wasn't embodying the rider's high. The show ring left me feeling exposed, vulnerable, and somewhat of a failure. My perfectionism was killing my passion.

At first, I had tried to overpower the horse with more equipment, harsh bits, overchecks, whips, and more. Then with frustration growing, I decided the best thing to do was sell Charisma. I couldn't look at myself anymore, and I felt like I was harming the horse's spirit.

I agonized over what to do next. I found myself in a familiar space: Do I keep Charisma or let her go? When I allowed my deepest thoughts to surface, I found myself saying things like, "I just can't get myself to cut the invisible ties between her heart and mine," and "How did this horse weasel her way into my heart?"

I had always been able to barricade myself from listening to that part of me. I was trained that success in life happens with control, trusting what you've been taught, attacking life head on, and trying harder. It certainly wasn't about surrendering to the unknown.

Yet somewhere . . . somehow . . . something had shifted in me. In the end, I choose that oh-so-subtle prompting of my heart over my training. I brought Charisma home.

At first, I felt paralyzed by my decision to keep her—after all, the strategies that I had held to so fiercely, all my skills and techniques I had used successfully on my previous horses, weren't enough. Charisma was asking me for something more, something deeper. She was asking me to retrain and reprogram myself. I chose to follow the horse.

I began to show her more of who I was, exposing my weaknesses and deepest thoughts. The more I did so, the more Charisma showed me who she was. The communication between us continued to deepen. As I became more self-aware, I could feel my personality soften and loosen. My empathetic abilities emerged more fully and I learned to trust my instincts.

This practice of learning to be present increased my ability to feel my body and my ride. No longer was I focused single-mindedly on the result; my concern was to support my horse emotionally and spiritually. I became aware of even the subtlest language: an ear twitch, a look or a thought that passed between us. An intuitive channel opened; not only were our bodies connected but our emotions and minds. I would instantly know what she was feeling or thinking. Her consciousness was growing right alongside mine.

We intimately came to know each other, with neither being the official leader. She became my muse, and I had a deep trust in her knowing my heart's true desire. We developed a spirit connection, two souls becoming one—just like with me and my sister. Charisma taught me that horses are great teachers when it comes to developing a connection to soul and spirit. It is our human vulnerability that resists this journey towards authenticity.

I now understand the full impact of my dream. It was validation that Charisma was sent to me from the Divine to remind me of who I am. It was the start of my spiritual journey, led by this horse, which created the work of my life. In remembering who I am, I believe that my sister on the other side has also benefited . . . allowing her to remember who she is.

Charisma is 30 years old now and what a journey it has been. We've shared many outstanding performances and memories in our three decades together, but my wholeness and connection to Spirit are the ultimate blue ribbon.

Nancy Proulx

LIZARD'S TRANSFORMATION

*T*ree-dwelling lizards called brown anoles are non-native to southwest Florida where I live. Anoles are so plentiful that they scurry out of the way when I walk down the sidewalks in my neighborhood. I see them sunning themselves on my patio furniture and window sills. They hang out on my porch and climb up my plants. I've even seen their brown heads peeking out of my bird houses.

The babies are my favorite. My heart sings when I see these little ones. Their bodies don't quite look solid and the slightest movement makes a rippling motion through their whole being. They are delightful.

One balmy summer evening, I was in the kitchen with my partner. Our talks frequently turned into arguments. That night, it escalated into yelling and telling each other to move out.

Flustered, I took a step backwards and felt a sickening *pop* under my foot. I knew without looking that a baby anole had gotten into the house and found its way across the tile floor. I felt so bad! It was still slightly moving so I gently picked it up and carried it outside.

I sat cross-legged on the deck, the halfmoon shining overhead. Crickets chirped and other insects buzzed in the distance. The noise made the air feel even thicker. The anger at my partner dissipated in the night air and all I felt was sadness and compassion for the lizard.

"I'm so sorry, I'm so sorry, I'm so sorry," I cried. The words became a comforting mantra.

As I watched over the anole, my thoughts turned to my own situation. My relationship was ending. It was messy. It was cruel. In an odd way, I felt like this lizard—the tender parts of me crushed. I knew it was time for me to go.

I continued to sit vigil on the deck, lost in thought. I wondered what really happens when we come across injured animals. *Do they come to us for help or to give us help? We give them medical help when we can, but they offer us spiritual medicine. They open our hearts. They help us reconnect to the rest of nature. Ironically, they often bring out our humanity.*

In those moments, I felt that this encounter was orchestrated, like somehow the brown lizard and I were co-creating this experience together. I focused my attention back on my messenger friend—its body was still slightly twitching but something had changed. Intuitively, I knew that the lizard's soul had left its body. It had died.

Surprisingly, I felt its energy rise and become one with the eucalyptus branch a few feet overhead. It further expanded and melded with the night sky. Then it became one with the stars, seeming to pull them closer in from the heavens to the right here and now. The air was alive with this energy and we were both a part of it.

Knowing it has passed, I picked up the lizard's body and held it. I felt inspired to honor it with song—the chorus of "Deep Peace of the Running Wave." I found a resting spot for it among the flowers at the edge of the deck . . . and with that . . . I closed my eyes and let it go.

A dark-haired man dressed in a light jacket appeared to me. I felt love pouring from his warm eyes and into my heart. He crouched down and took both my hands. Then he reached out and brushed the bangs off my forehead, like a father comforting his daughter.

"It was time," he said . . . and then he was gone.

Now bathed in peace, I lingered in the garden. Everything was incredibly alive and vibrant. I watched with simple fascination as two snails randomly made their way across a large leaf, antennae slowly moving. Their tiny bodies glistened and the slime they exuded sparkled in a trail behind them. After a long while, I went back in the house, transformed, knowing what I needed to do.

Anne Cederberg

SPIRIT OF THE HORSE

*O*ur beautiful newborn son Samson came and went from this world in one day—December 21, 2012.

As we gently dressed Samson, laid his tiny body in a special white box, and braced our hearts to let him fly home free, it felt like the world had unhinged. Consumed with grief, I was barely able to function or talk.

I couldn't bear to leave Samson behind in the hospital's clinical environment. We wanted to show him how loved he was and share with him what would have been his home. Nestled in his white box, we drove him around our village, and the first stop was to see the horses that bring us such joy. We spoke to Samson of all the fun he would have had being brought up in nature, surrounded by horses.

From that day onward, I was no longer who I had been. Something had died in me. *So, who am I now?* That became a precipice I clung to when I felt most out of control. My horses knew, and they were about to crack open and heal my broken heart.

About three months after the loss of Samson, I was led into the multisensory world by Donner, my four-legged energy healer. By this time, I had all but given up my former goal-oriented dreams. I hadn't had the energy or the fight to push myself. On this particular day with Donner, I was primed for surrender. As this beautiful creature read my emotions through empathic awareness, another grief swept in mixing with my original grief. I looked in Donner's eyes . . . and I let go.

Lost in this beautiful place of surrender, I could feel the pulse of Donner's heart match my own as it raced in sheer intrigue and breathtaking wonder. Gallant and brave, Donner danced in unashamed glory before me as an explosion took place in my mind. I kept following the explosions of light until suddenly I was looking into clear, still water. Something deep within me was being unleashed. Apprehensive at what was to be revealed, a flood of fear rushed through my veins.

Let go, Donner encouraged. *It's safe to look.*

Fear wasn't going to hold me back. I was determined to not let down my courageous equine guide, who was uncovering the mask I wore so well. Feeling exposed and vulnerable, I cried as I viewed myself though my horse's vision. I allowed myself to fall deeper into the ocean of love shimmering behind Donner's eyes. My identity crashed like waves cutting into the sea bed. Realization after realization of my misguided, self-indulgent thoughts and actions tumbled forth.

My mind couldn't comprehend all that was taking place and neither could it keep up. Intuiting that my disbelief was, at times, too much for me to handle, Donner would gently nudge my back and lower her head in acknowledgement of my release into freedom and Divine wisdom. Then her heart and mind showed me how to discover the life that waited. I could barely breathe as we raced together in her life-giving waters. I felt expanded while simultaneously held by the stunning mare's promise and honesty. I experienced God as this majestic nutmeg mare merged with all of me. We became one.

In the coming days and months, I continued to work with Donner and my other horses—Remedy, Billy, Revel, Cookie, and others. I was their humble student and was in awe of these great creatures who were willing to gift me with their wisdom. They were like magicians conjuring mind-clearing experiences that allowed my heart to bloom into all corners of my being. As my soul basked in the pleasures of this camaraderie, they pushed my developing awareness to take the next step. With no judgment, the horses drew from me all that I needed to release. The art of their unconditional love washed every cell of my being, slowly quenching a lifelong yearning to know peace.

Over time, they took me higher and higher into the embrace of the Divine. As I looked beyond Donner's shining, smooth coat, I saw waves of gold coiled, gleaming crystals of power waiting to be channeled back into my heart. This was God's message—that He is there at all times whenever I need him. No sooner did this thought come when it was extinguished by a burning flame from within. He had never left. God was in my heart!

No thought could usurp the awesome projection of love, joy, and wisdom that was transmitted to me from the horses. They've taught me how to respond rather than react to my fears. Nothing in their world is viewed as good or bad. Nothing can enter but love.

My four-legged angels brought me back to life and unshackled the chains I had woven around myself.

You have looked into the soul of the great and the mighty, the Divine power, the truth, my mare told me.

As my nutmeg beauty Donner walked towards me after several intense rounds of our recent healing work together, her face held an expression of peace like I had not seen before. Gentle yet powerful, she let out a sigh and dropped her head in front of me. Tears rolled down my face as the herd gathered around us. We stood together in silence, only the sound of birds and gentle breeze reminding us that we are physical beings.

Helen Brennand

DODDLE'S GIFTS

*O*nce upon a time, a fairytale is told to a little girl with solemn eyes. It's a beautiful story about how on Christmas Eve, humans are able to understand the animals. For on that holy night, the animals are given the gift of language.

Her heart is filled with wonder and joy. She desperately wants to hear the animals speak, so she stays awake through the night, hoping to witness this miracle. Year after year, Christmas Eves come and go, yet still she waits. Eventually, she banishes her longing to speak with animals and writes it off as mere fiction.

. . . And now here I am, many years later, experiencing this two-way communication as real, not make believe, through the beauty of a feline.

Doddle was my parent's cat for many years. One day, they brought him to live at my home on the Dutch sea coast. Doddle didn't know me very well and I had no clue about his food preferences and daily rhythms. Although we were not at ease with each other in those early days, we muddled through and respected each other. I knew, for example, that Doddle habitually left the house through the cat flap around 2:30 a.m. and returned around 4.30 a.m.

One day, after months of living together, Doodle was lying on his favorite window seat, soaking up the sun, and watching the world pass by. I sat down next to him.

"Well, Doddle," I said frankly, "we are stuck with each other. You are my responsibility. I will do all I can to provide you with a good home and all that you want. I promise this for better and worse, until one of us passes over."

I must have sounded very determined because Doddle raised his head and looked me straight in my eye. Something changed in his expression. He glanced thoughtfully at me and physically nodded. Through my claircognizance, I heard him mumble, *Okay, I am so glad to hear this.*

He sighed deeply and from that moment forward, his attitude turned around like a leaf on a tree. To say I was flabbergasted is putting it mildly. Doddle finally understood that he wasn't a guest who's overstayed his welcome, but that he belonged with me.

Everything changed that day, as I was finally able to hear the animals speak. Going forward, Doddle became my mentor and teacher, the cat of my soul. He possessed the power to make himself perfectly clear to me. He assisted me in developing my intuitive skills. We became so aligned that whenever I needed him to come in the house, I would simply think something like, *Sweetie, it's time to come home* and five minutes later, I'd hear the cat flap. Day after day, he took me by his paw and subtly prepared me to re-own my ancient wisdom, as well as my connection to the animal kingdom and the Divine.

Doddle told me that all animals, in physical or spirit form, carry messages for us humans. They help us become aware of our habits and challenges. They provide us with knowing when the time has come for us to dive deep into our subconscious to uncover and transmute what is holding us back—so that our most brilliant self is freed to bubble to the surface and catch light. When we do this, Doddle instructed me, not only are we able to elevate on our soul's path but the animals, too, are free to more brightly emanate their soul light.

Doddle decided to pass over on All Hallow's Eve about five years ago. He suffered for several years with a debilitating immunity inflammation disease that caused him pain in his throat and mouth. I asked him to give me a very clear sign when his time was near.

He kept his promise. Doddle seemed determined to use his last few steps before his hindlegs totally collapsed to visit his garden and smell the plants. Then we drove him to the vet, wrapped in his favorite blanket. For the first time in 17 years, he appeared to enjoy going on a car ride. Peering out the window along the way, he seemed to be saying goodbye to all the wonder and beauty of this beautiful earth, his eyes radiating trust, love, and serenity.

As he took his leave in style, the bright light that he was exploded from his body and enveloped and filled me with profound joy. In life, Doddle made it possible for me to welcome a whole new expression of myself, align with my life's purpose, and serve the Divine as an animal communicator and shamanic practitioner. And yet, at his passing, he saved this greatest gift for last.

Florentine Bisschops

THE HEALING POWER OF DONKEYS

I arrived at my friend's Colorado ranch for a weekend workshop, still deeply grieving the loss of my beloved horse, Lindsey. She had passed away a few weeks earlier and my heart was tender.

During a lunch break on the first day, I felt a strong call to sit with the donkey on the property (appropriately named Donkey). I pulled up a stool then Donkey walked over and stood in front of me, as though he knew the heartache I was enduring.

Tears poured down my face as I opened to my grief. When I bent forward on the stool, Donkey stepped in closer and wedged his neck around my body. It was quite possibly the best hug I've ever received.

I felt the grief of missing my mare slowly dissipate, as though Donkey was pulling it out of me and extracting all the pain. It's been said that donkeys carry both our belongings and burdens. In those moments, I knew this to be true. My grief was not just shedding in layers; it was being completely unwound.

After several minutes of this healing exchange, I started to wonder if others had just witnessed this animal's superpowers. I looked up and realized that we were alone in the arena. Donkey's eyes bore into my soul and I thanked him profusely. I tried to find some grass to give to him and he stepped back slightly.

You don't need to give me anything in return; you only need to receive, he conveyed.

As an equine-partnered life coach, I witness the healing power of horses all the time and had always judged donkeys as "less than" because I thought they're not as majestic, beautiful, and powerful. I was sorely wrong! I experienced such a deep clearing from Donkey that it deeply humbled me to experience his true gifts. In that moment, I resolved to share my newfound understanding of donkeys with others through my work.

I walked back to the tepee where the class was being held. I was a different person! As I entered the tepee, several people immediately noticed my transformation.

"You're glowing!" one said.

"I can feel your open heart and the love present," another commented.

I felt blissed out and completely cleansed, as though my soul had been restored to its true nature.

That afternoon, the class was led through a shamanic journey to find our power animal. I knew that donkey was mine for the coming year.

I ended up moving to Colorado just a few miles from this ranch, so I've been able to sit with Donkey again and witness his powerful healing ability. On one occasion, I had a kundalini experience in which my energy shifted into a vibration of pure bliss, connecting me to all beings. I remain in awe of how powerful Donkey (and all donkeys) can be and how much his energetic mastery affected my own. He taught me to just be and receive.

Kate Neligan

WHALE ENERGY

We set out on a beautiful yet slightly windy day in Monterey Bay, California. I was excited and curious to be on this research vessel, participating in a whale-watching excursion. After a while at sea, we spotted two types of dolphins running with a group of whales. It was exciting to behold their power and beauty.

My intuition nudged me to "talk" to the whales, so I walked to the front of the boat and stood there with my left palm facing down at the ocean. An incredible tingling energy went through me. Some type of connection was being made. I remained there for a while, filled with awe and unconditional love surging through my body. It was so magical that I spoke directly to the ocean: "I love you! I am so blessed by you!"

As we cruised along, I followed the energy of the whales and the dolphins, mimicking their movements with the palm of my hand as they swam and dove around us. Such joy! I intuited when and where the whales and dolphins would dive and resurface. They would emerge from the water exactly where I was holding my hand, as if following the energy.

The trip continued on as we trolled from one spot to another watching whale activity. On our last stop, we saw a mother and baby whale. The joyful energy intensified as the baby flipped from side to side. The communication between the whales and me continued, and I sensed when the baby was done playing and when the whales would be moving to another location.

A year later, I received news of an opportunity to return to Monterey Bay. My left hand tingled when I thought about going on this second whale watching trip. As I walked on the beach the evening before the excursion, I could feel the whale energy out in the ocean and could pick where they were.

Welcome back, I heard them lovingly communicate.

When we set out early the next morning, our vessel was surrounded by a species of seal that does not typically come into the harbor. It seemed as if they were escorting us out to sea . . . and then they were gone.

As the boat ferried us out across the waves, I glanced back at the shoreline and did a double take. *Could it be?* I couldn't believe my eyes! I was experiencing an open-eyed vision of a mythical creature called a Japanese *Bake-kujira,* or ghost whale. She had been waiting for me just above the water, translucent and so beautiful.

The ghost whale communicated to me that she had been protecting that body of water and was waiting for me to release her. I assured her that she was free to transition . . . and with that, she vanished.

This sea voyage gifted me with the opportunity to reunite with these gentle, ancient wisdom keepers. They reminded me about the song of the ocean, the playfulness of life, and of our innate connection to the Divine.

Lisa M. Jones

TURUL, MY SPIRIT GUIDE

In the Hungarian tradition, the mythical bird Turul—typically depicted as a hawk or falcon—is one of a protector Spirit. It is a special spirit guide for my native country and for me personally. Whenever I need help with making a decision, a hawk will usually appear.

Part of my life's work is passing on the ancient traditions and long-forgotten gifts of the Huns. Not long ago, I was pondering if I should stay on this path of teaching. This day, I saw a hawk on a tree branch close by and felt inspired to sing a special Hungarian song to him. He watched me and listened as I sang these words:

> *Hawk, fly up to the Sun into the blue sky*
> *and carry our proud song with you.*
> *Hawk, fly down from the Sun to the Earth*
> *and bring our Father's blessings with you.*

As I sang the words "fly down to the Earth", the hawk opened his wings and flew to the ground right next to my feet. I felt overwhelmed with gratitude by this very obvious and gracious connection.

The hawk stayed there until I finished singing, then flew to a nearby fence. I said my goodbyes and thanked him for his guidance. He took one last piercing look at me. By the time he flew away, I knew what I needed to do.

Szilvia Bartha

COOPER'S HAWK

*O*ur life was simple, complete, and filled with joy and love. All three of us—my wife Sara, our son Cooper, and myself—loved the outdoors and have always felt very connected to Mother Earth.

On April 13, 2011, our life drastically changed without warning when Cooper tragically lost his life in a terrible accident. A woodpile tumbled onto him and ultimately claim his life force.

Sara and I had never really put much thought into the spirit world or "the other side" yet we never discounted it either. At that time, our faith in God had completely vanished. We were swept away in our grief, trying to adapt to a life without our only son.

Over time, we met several people who introduced us to a new way of looking at life and encouraged us to seek answers. We were desperate to find our son on the other side. We vowed that if we could not have him in the physical world, we would do absolutely anything in our power to connect with him in the spirit world.

Thus, our journey began. Our faith in God, Spirit, or whatever you want to call it would return to us but not in the way we expected. We were encouraged to open our minds and hearts, and welcome the soul of our child into our lives.

As we grew together spiritually, we began to find our way, living life the best way we knew how. Our perception on life changed dramatically and we welcomed it.

About four months after Cooper's transition, I was driving home from work and couldn't get Cooper off my mind. This wasn't unusual, as I would talk to my son every chance I got. This particular day, I was feeling a bit disconnected, lonely for my son. I graciously asked Cooper to please send us a sign to let us know that his spirit is near and with us.

As I drove onto my driveway, I stopped my truck in complete amazement. Standing before me was a red-tailed hawk. I got out of the truck and something told me to sit down and extend my hand to the bird. The hawk started to walk toward me and sat just inches from my hand. I couldn't believe it! The bird was most certainly not afraid of me and I was not afraid of him. In those moments, we were just two souls sitting on a gravel driveway, staring at each other in awe.

I suddenly had the thought to grab a camera to document the encounter. I carefully got up and grabbed my phone out of my truck. I called Sara and told her to come to the end of the driveway, then I took a bunch of photos. I thought to myself, *Either this hawk is injured or it has prey nearby.*

As Sara approached, the hawk flew into a tree. Sara was blown away by its beauty and immediately felt it was a sign from our son.

"We have a book that talks about the spirit of animals and what they represent," Sara said. "Let's research Hawk."

With the hawk still in a nearby tree, we went into the house and paged through the book. What we discovered nearly knocked us off our feet.

A red-tailed hawk is a messenger from the spirit world and is also referred to as a Cooper's Hawk. Looking at each other with utter amazement, we immediately understood that this was our son's way of communicating with us. It was truly one of the greatest gifts we could have received from our beloved Cooper.

The hawk stayed around our home for a total of five days. All of our family members got to come in contact with it. After the very last family member saw him, the hawk moved on.

As for the two of us, we will forever be thankful to have felt the energy of our baby once again through the Spirit of Hawk. We know now that Spirit is real and palpable. In fact, Sara uses what we have learned from "the other side" to help others heal their hearts from the trauma of losing a loved one. We are incredibly grateful for Hawk as we continue to hold the spirit of our son close to our hearts.

Dr. Dan and Sara Beaupre

COYOTE MEDICINE

feel blessed to live in a pleasant neighborhood in Dana Point, California, with my wife, Jesseca, two stepdaughters, Serena and Ari, and Jesseca's mother, Sharon. With two dogs, two cats, two desert tortoises, one box turtle, and two chickens, everyone here obviously loves animals and we are honored to be stewards to these beings.

One day, my yellow Labrador Retriever, Sampson, and I were taking our usual walk through the community, ending up in the park, as we often do, just as dusk was settling in. I love the twilight hour when dark and light merge into a translucent veil that covers the land; the sky transforms from light-blue to a purple haze with splashes of reds, oranges, and yellows that trail the sun on its brief foray into the underworld.

As Sampson and I meander on the ribbon of sidewalk that snakes its way throughout the park, he wanders here and there, sniffing out remnant scents of those who had just been on the path. Suddenly, I sense something—an undefinable motion on one side of the park that borders the street, sidewalk, and fence. Instinctively, I turn in that direction, and within seconds, I make out something in the shadows trotting along the street. A lost dog? As I track the movement, it becomes apparent—it is a coyote!

I knew that coyotes lived and hunted in the canyons on two sides of my neighborhood, and occasionally wandered out into the streets and backyards, but I'd never witnessed one in the eight years we've lived here. I also know that local residents have seen coyotes; they post sightings on an app called The Neighborhood, along with notes about coyotes taking little critters like rabbits and cats. Coyotes are stealthy and often hunt under the cover of darkness. Occasionally we can hear them yipping somewhere in the canyons, as if they're having a celebratory party. They also have a reputation for being tricksters, and are able to use deception as a means of tracking their prey, such as one coyote chasing the prey into the jaws of another that is waiting close by in the shadows.

And now, here I am, face to face with one. I'm in a state of awe, as I frequently am when I come in touch with a wild animal that is still making a go of it, in spite of human intervention into what was once their territory. I feel right away that this animal is a messenger from Coyote Spirit, which was now making me conscious of the physical coyote in order to get my attention. It has my full awareness now, and I feel very safe even though we are only about 25 feet apart.

I pause in my tracks and allow Sampson to continue his roaming about, while I focus on the coyote. Before my eyes, he transforms into Coyote Spirit, the collective consciousness of *all* coyotes, calling to me from the being that has just appeared in my sight. Coyote Spirit is here to offer me a message through this four-legged, furry creature.

I prepare to receive Coyote medicine by taking a few slow, deep breaths, releasing any barriers to openly receive whatever Coyote has to tell me—whether through my eyes, ears, physical sensations, or my intuition (which is a knowing without knowing how you know).

Hearing my inner voice and body sensations are the two primary ways that I typically perceive and receive messages from Spirit. So, I hear this message, loud and clear, through my conscious awareness:

Beware! There is some trickery and deceit that you have to attend to. Someone you thought was a friend is deceiving you, acting friendly while betraying your trust.

I pause for a few seconds, contemplating this startling message, which continues as I watch the coyote trot down the street and disappear into the canyon.

Do you see how I'm somewhat veiled in the shadows of nightfall? You are barely able to see me, but your senses told you to look. This is how this friend is operating: not letting you see all of what's going on. You must pay much closer attention to what he does rather than what he says.

It's a tendency for you to trust first and ask questions later, Steven, and this has hurt you in more than just this situation. You know who this person is, but you have been unwilling to confront him for fear of losing his so-called friendship and being a "nice guy" . . . yet you must do so or you will experience even greater harmful consequences.

I am taken aback by this message, yet something is telling me that it's true, and I need to take heed of what Coyote Spirit is conveying.

As I begin to walk back to the house with Sampson, I contemplate what has been communicated. Three people come to mind, but only one that makes logical sense. He is not only a friend of 25-plus years, but also my accountant and financial adviser . . . yet now the seed of suspicion has been planted by Coyote.

In a flash, it becomes clearly obvious that this man, who I will call Dave (not his real name), is the person Coyote is referencing. I think back on my relationship with him as I continue trekking back home, Sampson faithfully by my side.

About seven years prior, I had loaned Dave a substantial amount of money for an investment he was making, plus an additional amount that would be my investment in the same project. There were detailed and signed agreements outlining the payments he was to make monthly, both as repayment for the loan and returns on my investment with him.

For the first four years, he faithfully made the payments, then they gradually became less regular and eventually stopped altogether. Whenever I'd ask about it, Dave would explain that there had been some setbacks; and me, being the nice guy (which Coyote nailed me on) and not wanting conflict, I went along with the increasing delays in getting the agreed-upon payments. After all, he is a friend . . . or so I thought. Coyote's wisdom obviously made me wonder how a friend could do something like this to a friend.

The more I thought about it on my walk that day, the angrier I got. Since I was obviously allowing myself to be manipulated by his appeal to our friendship when I would bring it up, there was a discrepancy in what he said and what he did (again, Coyote pointed this out).

So instead of continuing to stay angry, I took Coyote's advice to heart and consulted an attorney, one with a great reputation for dealing with these types of issues. Though what the attorney said made sense, I hesitated because I didn't really want to initiate a lawsuit with Dave. Besides, at that point, in spite of the mounting evidence, I still considered him a friend. At that point, I decided to defer any legal action.

Another two years went by and the situation only got worse. Still no payments. It forced me to revisit what Coyote had directly pointed out to me that day when I saw the coyote in my neighborhood. I began to look at these shadow elements in myself—the nice guy image, the desire to avoid conflict, misplaced loyalty—and realize that although I wasn't a victim, I had not made the appropriate moves to get ahold of what was rightfully mine. Perhaps the biggest revelation was that I had to come to the realization that Dave was really not my friend . . . at least, not any longer.

Eventually, I returned to the attorney and with his legal advice and knowledge, initiated a lawsuit. We ultimately ended up mediating the settlement, and though it wasn't quite what he owed me, I was completely satisfied with the outcome.

I wonder, at times, what would have happened—what further damage would have been done—had I not encountered and ultimately acted on Coyote's message that day. I was—and still am—so grateful that Coyote Spirit and the coyote in my neighborhood showed up to spark these revelations, which not only helped me immensely with these "outer world" concerns but also taught me a great deal about how I show up *in* the world.

I'm still not a fan of conflict, but because of Coyote's dose of medicine, it feels a lot more natural to stake my territory and stand up for what is rightfully mine—while still being a nice guy!

Dr. Steven Farmer

PART THREE

*Deepening Your Connection
with Spirit Animals*

For the animal shall not be measured by man. In a world older and more complete than ours, they are more finished and complete, gifted with extensions of the senses we have lost or never attained, living by voices we shall never hear.

They are not brethren, they are not underlings; they are other Nations, caught with ourselves in the net of life and time, fellow prisoners of the splendour and travail of the earth.

—HENRY BESTON

PRACTICES TO DEEPEN YOUR SPIRIT ANIMAL EXPERIENCES

Connecting with spirit animals is an ever-deepening process, as the bounty of the natural world is boundless in its innate intelligence and superpowers. The more you align with these sentient beings and allow them to work their magic in your life, you will begin to feel increasingly supported by these wild and wise allies, accompanied by a comforting knowing that you are never alone, and never have to go it alone. Support is all around.

When you encounter an animal that offers himself as a Divine channel for providing messages that guide you along your soul's journey, you will not only enhance your relationship with the animal world but also discover that you have more trust in the reality of Great Spirit. Realizing that there is another dimension to these amazing animal beings is life changing, as it affirms how intertwined we are with not only the animals but with *all* other life forms. You will recognize that Spirit can supply messages from other beings in the natural world as well, and that all the other spirits of nature are in abundant supply.

As your consciousness expands to incorporate these ways of receiving guidance, you will come to understand that, at any time, you can tune in and receive helpful information to support your purpose in being here on this amazing planet. During these dramatically changing times, it's critical that we do whatever we can to sustain a conscious relationship with Spirit. This chapter is dedicated to the ways in which you can commence your relationship with animal spirit guides and subsequently deepen it over time to encompass all of Life.

When it comes to solidifying your interrelationship with animal spirit guides, practice is key. Like most skills, it can best be honed through regular devotion and continued willingness to discover for yourself the power and magic of working with animals in this way.

PRACTICE DIRECT REVELATION

I recommend doing this as a very first step whenever you encounter a spirit animal in physical or etheric form. Direct revelation is another way of saying that you are engaging your inner senses. It simply means that there is no intermediary between you and the animal spirit guide. This is the purest and most immediate way to establish a connection and decipher what messages spirit animals are offering.

When an opportunity for learning about yourself is presented in the form of an animal spirit guide showing up—for example, you have a vivid dream about an octopus—close your eyes, take a deep breath, and review the dream or event. Tune in and telepathically ask Octopus Spirit, *Octopus, what's your message?* You can, of course, do this with any other being in the natural world— trees, clouds, mountains, and more; however, what I find is that information from animal spirit guides is the most accessible. You may find that you can relate more instinctually to animals than, say, Tree or Mountain Spirit. Experiment and observe yourself as you do.

Immediately after you've asked the spirit animal for its message, pay close attention to everything you receive and perceive. What do you see? What do you hear? What do you sense in your body? These perceptions could come in some or all of the ways outlined in Part One; for instance, you may hear with your inner voice and see images in your mind's eye, or your attention may be directed to look at or hear something in the external environment.

Perhaps when I encounter Elephant and ask him for the message, what I see is an image of an elephant raising his trunk. I may notice that he's standing in front of a wall then charging into it, the wall falling apart, and Elephant making his way through it.

So, I pause and contemplate what is just revealed to me. *Well, he's charging through a wall and the wall crumbles.* These visual metaphors convey a partial answer to the question. Then I hear with my inner voice, *You need to be less rigid with your beliefs and actions . . .* followed by, *You need to clean things up,* which I immediately realize is referring to "tidying up" a conflict I've just had with someone. The wall? Well, Elephant is encouraging me to not allow myself to be blocked in any way to achieving my goals, to break through my preconceived barriers, and even resolve any unfinished business that is standing in the way of my being able to forge ahead in life.

Of course, if you were to experience the same visual from Elephant, your interpretation might mean something slightly or completely different. If you're confused or uncertain about what the message means, go back and ask Elephant to clarify. Once again, close your eyes, take a couple of deep breaths, see the animal in your mind's eye, silently ask about the message, then pay attention to whatever shows up next, whether through images, words, sensations, thoughts, or some combination of these. The communication may be very clear or somewhat cryptic and dream-like, but however it shows up, this is your answer. Most importantly, trust what you get, even if it doesn't make immediate sense.

As another example of this concept of direct revelation, I'll offer a story of my encounter with a tortoise. I had journeyed across the country from Los Angeles to upstate New York to present a workshop at the Omega Institute about connecting with the spirit world. As I was driving along a somewhat twisty road on this unseasonably hot and humid day, suddenly I caught a glimpse of something on the pavement—a small, indistinct movement just ahead. As I approached, I could see that it was a tortoise. He had just crossed the dividing line and was moving from left to right, moseying along—naturally—at a tortoise pace, to the other side of the road. In the blink of an eye, I swerved and gratefully avoided running over this beautiful creature.

Once I had gotten over the initial shock, I realized that this little guy was still in danger, so I did a U-turn and tracked back to the scene of the crossing. I got out of the car and escorted him safely off the road. Standing there watching him amble into the forest, I closed my eyes and asked Tortoise Spirit what he was trying to tell me. His wisdom consisted of some simple messages that proved valuable not only for the class I was about to teach, but in other areas of my life at the time. In summary:

Slow down! You've got all the time in the world. Be willing to stick your neck out, take some risks. You are protected and cared for, and you can always retreat, if necessary. Know that help is always nearby when you need it—just put the word out. It will often show up in unexpected and surprising ways.

This was really helpful for me, since around that time I had just started offering random spirit animal readings, essentially tuning into individuals' animal spirit guides and relaying to them what was being communicated. Tortoise encouraged me to go for it, not hold back, trust the information I was getting, and pass it along confidently to the individuals for whom I was doing the readings. That weekend at Omega, I went on to teach the class and throughout, Tortoise's message continued to play itself out in various ways. My readings were sharp and detailed, thanks to the willingness on the part of the animal spirits to clearly show themselves to me. As I worked and saw a vision of Tortoise's shell in my mind's eye, he reminded me that I'm safe at all times, in spite of life whizzing by us, just like the cars whizzing by our friend on the road that weekend.

Direct revelation can come through physical sensations as well, such as muscle tension, spontaneous body reactions, tastes, or smells. I sometimes notice that my "fur" will stand up when I am in communication with spirit animals. One day as I was driving along and noticed a bull in a nearby pasture, I tuned into

Bull Spirit and asked for a message. Immediately, I took a deep breath and felt my chest expand. The sensation translated into my inner voice saying, *You can be proud of what you have achieved, so stand tall with your head up.*

In another instance, although I didn't see a skunk, I caught the distinct smell of one that had recently passed by. Skunk conveyed to me, *Pay close attention to anything right now that smells funny and keep your distance.* I recognized right away that he was referring to a couple of people at that time who were attempting to manipulate and take advantage of me. I thanked Skunk for his odorous reminder.

RESEARCH THE ANIMAL'S SPIRITUAL MEANING

Only after you've experimented inwardly with direct revelation do I advise taking the next step, which is to search outwardly for interpretations of spirit animals. Learn about your spirit animal as much as you can by reading material from reputable sources. There are a variety of books and oracle cards on the market that can be useful when you're starting to explore this path. For this reason, I've written my books, *Animal Spirit Guides, Pocket Guide to Spirit Animals*, and *Earth Magic*, as well as my oracle cards, *Power Animal Oracle Cards, Messages from Your Animal Spirit Guides, Earth Magic Oracle Cards*, and *Messages from the Spirits of Nature Oracle Cards.*

We live in a virtual world so of course there is plenty of information online. You can type phrases into the search bar such as "otter spirit animal", "buffalo animal spirit guide", "lizard spirit", or "eagle power animal", and you'll find an abundance of possible meanings and messages. As you peruse this information, stay in touch with your intuition and let it guide you to the resources that are the best ones for you at that time. As you read, notice the qualities and attributes of the animals that you feel drawn to.

Ponder how the animal's traits relate to you and how their characteristics might relate to what is happening in your life. Let's say you are guided to Lobster but you don't know why. Upon learning more about Lobster Spirit, you immediately resonate with its description as a solitary creature that has amazing powers of concentration. *Hmmm,* you think, *I also get snappy when I'm around others for too long, and I'm at my best when I'm submerging myself in my work for a length of time. I never thought about it but yeah, I have a natural affinity for that. Thanks, Lobster!*

As you research and learn about the meanings of each spirit animal, you can begin to understand that animal communication is a two-way street. Yes, animals will show up in your everyday life, and you can also proactively call on particular ones for help with specific needs. Suppose, for example, that you are faced with a challenging task and would like to have a greater sense of confidence to accomplish it. There are several animal spirit guides that you can engage with. Ask Cougar Spirit to give you the courage to stand up for yourself, and to take chances and risks. Invoke Peacock for help in overcoming your shyness and being willing to show your colors. Call in Chimpanzee's strength to help you access your intuitive problem-solving genius.

For a detailed list of Spirit Animals for Specific Purposes, see the Appendix at the end of this book.

OBSERVE THE ANIMAL AND ITS CHARACTERISTICS

If an animal comes into your environment in any way, pay close attention. It may be there for its own purpose, or it may have arrived just for you. Of course, most animals you encounter will be in a natural setting, such as in your back yard, the streets in your neighborhood, in your local park or in the woods where you hike. I encourage you to spend as much time as you can in the animals' habitat, as the wisdom they impart often sharpens and magnifies in nature.

When you encounter an animal in the wild or in your imagination during dreams or meditation, reflect on how you feel in the animal's presence. Are you in awe or scared? Are you happy to see the animal or do you feel threatened? Use all of your senses to intuit the roots of the emotional charge. Is someone in your life intimating you?

Notice what the animal is doing when you come into contact with it. Are the rabbits playing and chasing each other, or are the rams snorting and butting heads? Again, try to tie this back to what is occurring in your relationships. Observe if any new emotions or associations emerge, as they may have been outside of your awareness until now. The spirit animal could represent your feelings, but also a person, an event, or a situation from your past or present life.

Ask the animal to speak directly to you and deliver its message. A few years ago, while working in my office, I noticed the persistent chirping of a bird beyond my picture window. After a while of hearing its insistent cadence, I walked outside and saw a mockingbird at the top of an arbutus tree in my backyard. A second one flew to the top of the tree just as I was greeting the first one. They continued their raspy bellowing for some time.

The next day, each of the birds dive-bombed me in the backyard, and I realized that they must be protecting their babies. Deciding to investigate, I placed a ladder against the tree, climbed up a few steps and saw two baby mockingbirds tucked into a nest among the branches. Mama bird swooped at me to tell me she meant business and would fiercely protect her offspring. Telepathically, I assured mama mockingbird that I would not harm her babies. As I did, I got a sense that Mockingbird Spirit also had something that she wanted to communicate to me on a personal level.

Tuning in further, I received several messages that related back to the medicine that Mockingbird Spirit represents—that of helping you overcome struggles with self-expression, and finding your voice in a playful and inventive way. First, she conveyed how important it was for me to fight for what I believed was right by speaking my truth through my writings and teachings. Leading up to that day, I had been feeling shy about sharing my thoughts on some topics that may have been construed as controversial.

In those moments standing near the tree, Mockingbird emboldened me to carry on with what I knew in my heart I should do, including creating some products that help children develop their spiritual consciousness. She also reiterated a message that I get quite often from various spirit animals: *Sing, Steven, sing!* I had been neglecting playing my guitar and singing, so it was a reminder to return to my music for a least a few minutes every day.

I thanked Mockingbird for her wisdom that day and, before parting ways, sent her a message of my own: *Bless you! May you and your babies thrive!*

If your spirit animal shows up in a meditation or dream, employ the same principle here of observing the animal and being attentive to the messages it is delivering.

JOURNALING OR AUTOMATIC WRITING

Now that you've had a close encounter with the animal spirit guide through direct revelation, by researching its meaning, and by observing it in your dreams or waking state, the next step for delving into its wisdom is to write about it in the form of journaling or automatic writing. You may choose to work with one animal at a time.

With a blank piece of paper before you and a pen in hand, close your eyes, breathe slowly and deeply, and allow yourself to relax as much as possible.

Pose your question to any animal spirit guide that has called to you or gotten your attention. Begin to record your thoughts or allow your hand to start writing whatever words come through. Usually, your hand will feel somewhat disconnected from you. Don't force the writing; just be patient. Keep breathing slowly and comfortably.

Experiment with this multiple times and see what happens. You may be surprised at how well this can work. One thing you may notice is that these writings will have a slightly (or completely) different tone than your usual writing style.

Here's an example of direct revelation via automatic writing that I received from Raven several years ago.

As I fly upon this Earth, making my way across the land, I see nothing but beauty. It troubles us that you human beings are so focused on your fears. So many people are worried about this and that. The Creator of All that moves through us and as us with breath delights in both the dark and the light. Look at my blackness. Does that make you nervous? Does it challenge you, just like the shadows of humankind that show themselves to you in others and in yourself?

Welcome those shadows, for it is the light of awareness when shed upon them that, no, doesn't dissolve them, but just reveals what needs to be revealed. The shadows of addictions, greed, secrecy, righteousness, hate, envy—own them! Don't let them rule you, but own them. One of the gifts I as Raven Spirit bring is helping you bring those shadows into the Light to be integrated so you can more completely accept your humanity.

You people separate the light and the dark, thinking that it's somehow bad to be "in the dark." Yet do not fear the darkness in you or others. Embrace them and watch what happens. By accepting these very human characteristics, you find understanding and compassion. There but for the grace of the Creator go I. Often said, but not often felt deeply. Not out of arrogance or a holier-than-thou frame, but from a place of deep compassion for not only your fellow human travelers, but all travelers on this planet.

Grace. Finding peace in grace. What does that really mean? Means to be aligned with Spirit, to be at one with all these aspects, to truly feel in your heart of hearts, even if only moments at a time, the truth of who you are: intimately intertwined and connected to All That Is. You are the Creator. The Creator is you. You are Creation. Creation is you. You are all of the Creator and Creation, yet also only one small part.

Duality exists only in your mind. Unity exists in your heart.

TAKE A MEDITATION JOURNEY

Once you have researched the animal spirit guides that have crossed your path and have connected with them more directly through automatic writing, now it is time to truly meet and begin to work with them. Meditating with your spirit animal is a powerful way to do this and can be quite an elucidating experience. Doing a guided meditation is also the perfect way to bridge the subtle divide between the material and spirit worlds.

Review this meditation journey before trying it and do your best to follow the written guidance. You may wish to record it on your iPhone or other device and listen to it in your own voice, or ask someone else to record it for you. Another option is to do this meditation with a friend or group of friends, where one of you reads it then everyone discusses what comes up for them during the meditation.

Note that you'll be going to the lower world, which is an etheric area in the earth where the spirit animals reside. It's not at all the same as what we typically think of as the underworld. The lower world is a notion that has its origins in shamanic practices and is completely safe, although it's best to ask a favorite spirit animal or power animal, if you have one, to accompany you as a spiritual ally.

Doing this journey may or may not bring forth the animal spirit guide that you are expecting; even your power animal, if you have one, may send someone else. The spirit animal that does show up will be the one that's exactly right for your concern, so be open to whatever occurs. Okay, here goes.

Put on some relaxing ambient music, turn the lights down, and find a comfortable seated or lying down position. Take a couple of slow deep breaths. When you're ready, close your eyes. Take another deep breath, and when you let it out, relax. Know that you're safe at all times.

If you travel with a spirit animal or any other spiritual beings, call on them now to help you know you're safe . . . loved . . . protected . . . at all times. Take another breath and let your awareness track your breathing for the next few moments. Notice how relaxed and comfortable you feel now . . . letting go of all tension . . .. taking all the time in the world . . . allowing yourself to completely let go and you continue breathing.

Now let your consciousness gently and gradually float down, into the earth, into the lower world . . . dropping comfortably down into the earth . . . knowing all the while that you're completely safe and protected at all times. As you drop into the earth, notice the sensations in your body . . . notice your breathing . . . notice how relaxed you feel.

Now as you descend, soon you come to a grassy area. Observe how you float down until you land gently on your feet in this meadow, feeling comfortable and safe. As you arrive, look around you and see what you see . . . not too far away, a forest . . . and in the distance, the mountains . . . on the other side of the forest is the sea. Be aware of the colors . . . notice any sounds you hear. Be aware of any smells

. . . feel the pleasant warmth of the sun on your skin . . . perhaps you can feel a slight breeze.

You have a choice of staying in this beautiful meadow or wandering about to any of these other areas. Go ahead and make your choice and if it means walking to another area, do so. Take your time. If you stay in the meadow, go ahead and be seated in a comfortable place. If you wander to the mountains, the forest, by the river in the forest, or to the beach, once you arrive there, have a seat in a comfortable place. Take a deep breath and relax into the setting you're in, using all your senses.

Now think of your question. As you do, you soon notice an animal coming to you . . . and you realize it's an animal spirit guide. It's exactly the right one for the question you have in mind. It may or may not be your totem animal or power animal. It may or may not be one that you saw in a dream or a vision . . . but you feel confident that this is the right one for your purpose. You're completely safe, protected. This animal spirit guide comes up to you, very friendly and willing to help you out. You communicate your question telepathically to this spirit animal.

After you've done so, observe everything that immediately follows. The information may come as a visual image, something you hear, a feeling in your body, or a thought in your head . . . it may be cryptic or very direct and clear. No matter how it comes, just notice without trying to interpret. If something isn't clear, ask this spirit animal for further clarification. Take a few moments to pay attention to what is coming to you. Simply allow yourself to absorb the information.

Once that feels complete, turn to your animal spirit guide and thank them in some way. Notice now that this animal spirit guide gives you a small gift . . . it's a symbol of this journey, a small token of this spirit guide's love and care for you. When it's offered and you receive it, first hold it in your heart. Close your eyes and take a couple of slow, easy breaths . . . breathe it in . . . notice how it feels. Open your eyes and once again thank this spirit animal.

Say your farewells to each other. Your animal spirit guide departs, and once again you close your eyes. Now you feel yourself lifting up from the lower world back into the middle world . . . back to where you started from. Notice your breathing . . . you may want to wiggle your fingers and toes as you bring your awareness back into your body. Take your time . . . let your breath be relaxed and comfortable.

Whenever you're ready, open your eyes and look around at your surroundings. This will help to orient you to present time and third-dimensional reality. Once you're completely back, you may want to jot down some notes from this journey.

I encourage you to write out in your journal whatever happens during the meditation. The message you get from your animal spirit guide may be perfectly clear. If it isn't, just let it work you throughout the day or evening. Often, other pieces will begin to synchronistically come to you after doing this kind of journey. To supplement what you are getting intuitively, look up the characteristics of the animal for its relevant symbolic meaning.

Repeat the practice as often as you'd like in order to address any type of question or concern you have, knowing that your animal spirit guide will give you simple yet brilliant advice.

INTENSIFY YOUR STUDIES

After a while of having a consistent practice of automatic writing and meditation with your animal spirit guides, something magical eventually begins to happen. You will find yourself walking through your days in a more curious and reverent way towards all animals and sentient beings. These practices with your close animal kin will no doubt invoke in you a greater empathy and authentic compassion for others and for our living planet.

Speaking from experience, I can attest to the awe and wonder that animals will bring into your existence. They may change your mindset and world view completely, and for the better. You could feel lighter, calmer, and more patient, and will probably experience random moments of intense joy and gratitude. These are the side effects of animal medicine!

After a while of working with spirit animals on your own, you may be inspired to focus your practice even more by working with individuals who have an expertise in specific related fields of study. Over the past few decades, training in the areas of animal consciousness and spirituality have opened up and expanded more broadly. If you feel a resonance with this in your heart, I encourage you to follow your curiosity and intuition, and see where it leads you.

One avenue of pursuit could be to work with a shamanic practitioner. As mentioned earlier, individuals skilled in this ancient lineage and spiritual practice can do a shamanic journey on your behalf to find and retrieve your power animal—even, perhaps, initiate your long-term relationship with that spirit animal. They can also initiate a divination journey to a spirit animal who is identified as a teacher with a question that you have. The practitioner can also teach you how to perform a shamanic journey so that you can do these for yourself.

Another potential area of study and certification is the emerging field of animal communication. Training and teachers are available for those who wish to become an animal communicator, something more and more people are doing either professionally or for their personal use. With this skill, you will learn and put into practice the various ways to communicate directly with the animals, including through telepathy. There's no better way to give back to the animals than to learn their language.

If you have an affinity for horses, equine-assisted therapy is another option. This is where you work directly with a trained therapist on your self-development with assistance from the horse. It allows you to be up close and personal with these dynamic beings. In this kind of therapy, the horse steps into the role of energy healer, as horses are quite gifted at transmuting energy and mirroring the feelings of their handlers, riders, and those who come to them for this healing purpose. Horses are such powerful healers that the fields of complementary medicine and energy healing now include specialized equine therapy. You may even find yourself drawn to become an equine therapist or work in the field of equine-assisted learning.

The true blessing of these deeper practices and fields of study is that you will begin to listen with animal ears, see through animal eyes, feel through animal hearts, and think with the wisdom of our four-legged and winged brethren.

DANCE, SING, AND CELEBRATE WITH YOUR SPIRIT ANIMAL

The final step in merging with your spirit animal is through movement, sound, and full-out joy. While dancing and singing with your animal teacher may sound like fun and games—which it is, too—this activity can be soul stirring, as you are intertwining with the essence of the animal.

The heightened frequencies and coherency created through the art of music, drumming, chanting, and dancing will further open doors of perception and immersion into oneness with all animals and Great Spirit. It will happily cause you to lose all preconceived judgements that you may have acquired through societal norms that animals are less intelligent or worthy than us. You will feel them as the equal soul beings that they are.

Dress up in whatever ceremonial garb you have within reach, put on some music with a solid rhythmic component, invite your spirit animal to merge with you, then *allow the spirit animal to dance with you!* Let yourself completely let go and express your wild self. There are no rules here, as this is the realm of pure imagination and creativity. Don't be surprised if you begin to embody qualities of your spirit animal in your movements and vocalizations. Let your hair down and go for it!

Sing to your spirit animal as you dance. It can be a song that you know or a melody that comes to you intuitively. Or, ask your spirit animal to teach you a song. No talent or ability is required; this is about stepping outside the bounds of your human nature and into the quintessence of the animal.

When your joyful ceremonial time together is complete, unmerge from your spirit animal and give thanks to it.

Doing all of these practices and rituals consciously and conscientiously are a gracious way to give something in exchange for the gifts that the animals bring to you—which brings us to our final discussion about the principle of reciprocity.

EVOLVING OUR INTERRELATIONSHIP WITH ANIMALS

*I*n every relationship, there is an exchange. You get something and you give something back, and vice versa.

Typically, this is done automatically without much thought. You go to the store and exchange money for goods. You give your friendship to someone, no matter the dynamics of the relationship, and that person offers their friendship in return. You tend to your garden and receive a harvest of vegetables, fruits, or flowers. You feed and care for your pets and they respond with their companionship, appreciation, and love.

Yet when this universal concept of give-and-take is done with gratitude and conscious awareness, it elevates this ordinary exchange to a higher level of reciprocity. The principle of reciprocity is an especially important one when working with animal spirit guides, and it's important to honor them and their gifts of wisdom with an exchange. It's a shift in mindset from *What can the animals do for me?* to *What can I do for the animals?*

First, I'd like to say a word about objectification, as the language we use is essential in order for us to walk in the world in a more mature way with animals and other sentient beings. The English language is structured in such a way that we objectify the elements of the natural world. That beautiful oak tree becomes an "it" rather than a relative. The clouds in the sky are things rather than spiritual manifestations that imply a more intimate relationship with us. Other than domesticated animals, most other sentient beings become an "it" to us, sustaining the illusion of separateness.

I find it interesting that some other languages, such as French, Italian, and Spanish, designate other beings and objects with masculine and feminine references, which implies a greater sense of our relationship with them. Going a step further, in most Native American languages, the various elements of the natural world are named as relatives and elders—Grandfather Wind or Grandmother Ocean, for example, and from there, designations such as the Cloud People, the Tree People, the Plant People, and the Animal People.

I prefer this heartfelt verbal recognition that everything and everyone is a part of this vast web of life. What we receive from Earth Mother and all her children are tremendous gifts, and we should, as much as we can, enact the principle of reciprocity, even in the words we speak. To me, it is an essential element of working in this spiritual domain of animal spirit guides.

What can we do to be in a more evolved interrelationship with our animal friends? Following are some examples of ways to reciprocate the gifts of both the physical animals and their counterparts, the animal spirit guides.

SUPPORT ANIMAL CAUSES

For you, reciprocity might be donating to organizations that serve the animal kingdom, including the aviary and aquatic species. This is one way to honor the animals as our equals and put our dollars where our hearts are. I commit a percentage of my book royalties to specific nonprofits whose work I want to see advance. You might find it appropriate to tithe in a similar way.

If peaceable protest is your calling, this is another way to support those who don't have a voice and personally reconnect with the animal world as allies. My wife's mother, who lives with us, absolutely adores animals. Over the years, she has been an activist for the humane treatment of animals and has taken part in protests with PETA. I've witnessed first-hand the difference a single person can make in these efforts.

If you're not an activist, then consider donating your money, time, or energy to the animals, such as volunteering at or purchasing supplies for your local animal shelter. Of course, adopting animals is an act of love, but you can also temporarily take in a rescue pet as a foster parent.

BE AN ANIMAL STEWARD OR CARETAKER

Another way to create an exchange with the animal world is to become stewards or caretakers of the animals that come into our lives . . . however they end up with us. It could be something as simple as loving those two goldfish that your children wanted, or as involved as choosing a lifestyle of homesteading, where you raise chickens, goats, or horses.

If you find yourself caretaking an animal that is not as common as a dog or cat, such as a tortoise, rabbit, or a hamster, first learn as much as you can about that kind of animal so you can give it the best care possible. Always consider, from the animal's perspective, what is best for it.

It's possible to have domesticated animals even on a relatively small plot of land. My family and I have a small suburban plot of land, with—as I mention in my earlier story—two dogs, two cats, two chickens, and three desert tortoises. There is definitely a reciprocity going on here! In return, the gifts they provide to us are immeasurable.

Having pets is, of course, another way to steward animals. They can teach you about a different kind of love, one that includes yet transcends human love. They mirror to us patience, kindness, happiness, and a sense of humor and lightness. Our tortoises remind me to go at a slower pace and take periods of healthy hibernation. Pismo, my daughter's six-foot-long boa constrictor, became my pet for a few years after my daughter came of age and moved out. This magnificent being graced us with many fascinating experiences over the years. Pismo loved to wrap herself around me—and no, she didn't squeeze me to death and make a meal out of me! She was always gentle and loving, in exchange for the love we gave her.

Now, indulge me as I brag for a minute about my two wonderful dogs. Scout, about a year old, is rambunctious and gradually learning to socialize. He reminds me to be playful and not be so serious. Sampson, our seven-year-old yellow Labrador Retriever, is sweet, gentle, and has the soul of a therapy dog. I recall one time when I was working with a client family and had an appointment with their 14-year-old daughter. Sampson was lying in my office when the teen girl came in and sat down; within a couple of minutes, she had broken down in tears.

Right away, Sampson got up, went over, and put his head against her leg to comfort her. She stopped crying as she stroked his fur, enabling us to proceed with the session. Sampson didn't leave her side for several minutes until she was calmed down enough to talk about what was troubling her. He then returned to lying down but stayed close by—just in case.

PERFORM A SIMPLE HONORING

Anyone, anywhere can do a simple ceremony of thanks to the animals for their presence. For the ones directly in your charge, offer prayers of gratitude on a regular basis for their health and wellbeing. Simply thank Great Spirit for blessing them. Hold them, if you can, and speak the words "I love you." Express that love through action, such as playing with them, grooming them, or feeding them treats periodically.

For the wild ones, take care of these animals when they come your way. Again, learn all you can about what the animal might require in order to sustain itself, including having the right habitat, food, shelter, and safety from predators. If the animal you encounter appears to be injured or in distress, rescue it with help from your local animal shelter, wildlife rehabilitation center, or animal control agency. You can also call your local nature center in order to learn what you can do for the safety and health of the animal. Pray for its health and safety as it heals and reorients back into the wild.

These ways of demonstrating the principle of reciprocity with love and sincerity build the relationship with the animal kingdom, and the animal spirit guides that teach you. They are a blessing to have and behold, and deserve to be blessed in return.

FINAL THOUGHTS AND BLESSINGS

*W*e may have lost our way, but there is hope. Many more of us are sensing into and remembering that humans are merely one part of the natural world, and that we are deeply embedded in the glorious and intricate web of life. We are beginning to understand that a majority of the actions we have taken in our collective arrogance to dominate the planet has ultimately upset the delicate ecological balance of this world and is leading to our own destruction.

The partly well-intentioned reasons for these choices have been to make life as comfortable and convenient as possible—but mainly for humans. In the process, a massive illusion of separateness from the natural world has been created, which leads us to believe—quite falsely—that humans are the superior species. Every being on this planet, in its own way, has an intelligence—some that are even more refined and attuned than our own. And let's not forget that there is an even greater force operating in our lives: the all-knowing Great Spirit.

During these times of dramatic changes when fear and uncertainty can so easily be triggered by world affairs and personal challenges, it's more critical than ever that we have an anchor in our spiritual practices, as Spirit is the true guiding light that helps us navigate life's trials and successes. We can readily access the voice of Spirit by recognizing our kinship with the animals and allowing the Divine to speak through them. None of us need anything to do this; there is no barrier to entry, as animals are all around us, ready and willing to offer their medicine.

I hope that the stories in this book have provided both the encouragement and skills to receive the guidance, protection, and healing that is always available through animals as messengers of Great Spirit. Taking inspiration from them, I encourage you to explore these practices with an open mind and heart. I promise that doing so will anchor you firmly in the wisdom of Spirit as communicated through our animal friends.

Thank you for your love of the animals and your willingness to work with spirit animals as an important aspect of your consciousness path. Every one of us who is helping to reintegrate our connection to the other aspects of the sentient world is contributing in a positive way to our planetary evolution. In fact, I believe we are in the process of a massive awakening as a human race, one in which we will fully align with all of Life and honor all sentient beings as equal.

Blessings to you in this grand adventure called Life!

APPENDIX

Spirit Animals for
Specific Purposes

Specific spirit animals can be called upon for particular conditions or situations in which you may need help or support. Or, you may wish to establish or reinforce a quality or characteristic within your own makeup similar to those of an animal spirit guide.

For most situations, you'll have more than one choice of spirit animal, so whenever that's the case, I suggest that you intuitively choose which animal spirit resonates with you for that particular condition or quality. Then, using the meditations and techniques that I've outlined earlier in the book, call on them with reverence and gratitude for the wisdom they are about to impart.

Once you've done this, you may get an immediate sign or result, but more likely, you'll receive further guidance and direction as to how to alleviate the condition, or ways to bring out more of the characteristics that you want to exhibit.

ABUNDANCE AND PROSPERITY
Buffalo
Cow
Crane
Deer (White-tailed)
Dragon
Elk
Frog
Gnu
Jaguar
Kangaroo (Grey Kangaroo)
Kingfisher
Ladybug
Puffin
Python
Rat
Salmon
Seal
Swallow
Turkey
Turtle
Walrus
Whale
Woodpecker

ACCEPTANCE OF OTHERS
Dragon
Hawk

ACCEPTANCE OF SELF
Duck (Wood Duck)

Hedgehog

Moose

ACCEPTANCE OF NEW IDEAS AND POSSIBILITIES

Dragon

Monkey

Wasp

ADAPTABILITY AND FLEXIBILITY

Cheetah

Chimpanzee

Dingo

Duck

Fox (Red)

Goshawk

Hare

Hawk

Hummingbird

Kite

Magpie

Polar Bear

Raccoon

Rat

Road Runner

Seal

Starfish

ADDICTIONS, HEALING

Bear

Rattlesnake

Snake

Tarantula

AFFECTION, GIVING AND RECEIVING

Baboon

Chimpanzee

Cockatoo

Mole

Moth

Quail

Sandpiper

Scorpion

Sparrow

Walrus

Wolf

AMENDS, MAKING

Alligator

Cassowary

Chimpanzee

Hedgehog

ANGER MANAGEMENT

Condor

Coyote

Dove

Kinkajou

Kite

Skunk

Swan

Whale

Wombat

ANXIETY AND FEAR, CALMING

Bat

Egret

Kingfisher

Kite

Polar Bear

Snake

Spider

Squirrel

APPEARANCES, PERCEIVING WHAT'S BEHIND

Anteater

Ferret

Gopher

Hare

Hippopotamus

Owl

Rhinoceros

Seal

Shark

Snow Leopard

Starfish

Weasel

APPRECIATION OF NATURE AND THE ENVIRONMENT

Chipmunk

Gibbon

Goat

Gorilla

Hummingbird

Kiwi

Road Runner

Seagull

Unicorn

Wolverine

Woodpecker

ASKING FOR WHAT YOU WANT

Armadillo

Bear

Goat

Polar Bear

Sparrow

Weasel

ASSERTIVENESS

Bear

Cougar

Great Horned Owl

Jaguar

Komodo Dragon

Otter

Parrot

Polar Bear

Raccoon

Skunk

Sparrow

Weasel

Wolverine

Wombat

AUTHORITY, ESTABLISHING OR MAINTAINING YOUR
Jaguar
Lion
Moose
Shark
Skunk
Wolverine

AUTONOMY AND INDEPENDENCE, SUPPORT FOR YOUR
Chipmunk
Falcon
Heron
Hummingbird
Lynx
Moose
Orangutan
Owl (Screech Owl)
Sloth
Tiger
Wasp
Zebra

AUTONOMY AND INDEPENDENCE, SUPPORTING OTHERS IN THEIR
Falcon
Moose

BALANCE, REGAINING OR MAINTAINING
Black Widow Spider
Chinchilla
Crane
Goat
Grebe
Jaguar
Kangaroo
Magpie
Orangutan
Orca
Ram
Seal
Snow Leopard
Spider
Whale
Zebra

BALANCING INTELLECT AND EMOTIONS
Barn Owl
Dragonfly
Flamingo
Goat
Magpie
Seagull
Spider
Wasp
Woodpecker

BALANCING MASCULINE AND FEMININE ENERGIES
Deer
Emu
Loon
Magpie

Penguin

Sandpiper

Sea Horse

BEGINNINGS, NEW

Antelope

Buffalo

Bull

White Cockatoo

Cuckoo

Duck

Eagle

Goat

Ram

Robin

Salamander

Salmon

Squirrel

Stork

BEING FULLY PRESENT

Goshawk

Hedgehog

Hummingbird

Jaguar

Kangaroo

Komodo Dragon

Lion

Mockingbird

Parrot

Polar Bear

Raven

Rhinoceros

Whale

BLOCKAGES, CLEARING

Canary

Elephant

Robin

Squirrel

Toad

Whale (Blue Whale)

BOUNDARIES, SETTING CLEAR

Bear

Bull

Cassowary

Donkey

Gecko

Great Horned Owl

Groundhog

Grouse

Shark

Skunk

Sparrow

Wolf

BREATHWORK

Dolphin

Groundhog

Koala

CALM, REMAINING

Condor

Coyote

Crane

Kite

Musk Ox

Skunk

Swan

Whale

CHALLENGES AND STRUGGLES, OVERCOMING

Buffalo

Black Cockatoo

Condor

Eagle

Jellyfish

Musk Ox

Python

Robin

Salmon

Sandpiper

Swallow

Tiger

CHANGES, LIFE

Butterfly

Chimpanzee

Cuckoo

Gnu

Heron

Impala

Kinkajou

Kite

Komodo Dragon

Polar Bear

Python

Rattlesnake

Road Runner

Salamander

Seal

Snake

Sparrow

Spider

Swan

Tiger

Toad

Wombat

CHEERING UP

Bluebird

Meadowlark

Parrot

Swallow

CHOOSING YOUR WORDS CAREFULLY

Bee

Hyena

Komodo Dragon

Lark

Macaw

CLEARING UP MISUNDERSTANDINGS

Blue Whale

Seagull

Tasmanian Devil

Toucan

COMMUNICATION, CLEAR

Blue Whale

Chimpanzee

Chinchilla

Chipmunk

Cockatoo

Dolphin

Gecko

Giraffe

Gnu

Gorilla

Humpback Whale

Kingfisher

Loon

Magpie

Monkey

Orangutan

Seagull

Squirrel

Stork

Swan (Trumpeter Swan)

Tasmanian Devil

Wolverine

Wombat

CONFIDENCE, BOOSTING YOUR

Bull

Chipmunk

Cockatoo

Cougar

Egret

Gibbon

Kangaroo

Kingfisher

Owl

Peacock

Polar Bear

Ram

Raven

Skunk

Swan

Tiger

Toad

Zebra

CONFLICT RESOLUTION

Baboon

Beaver

Dolphin

Dragon

Gecko

Jellyfish

Moose

Robin

Zebra

CONFRONTING JUDGMENT OR NEGATIVITY IN OTHERS

Boar

Cuckoo

Elk

CONFRONTING YOUR FEARS

Gibbon

Jaguar (Black Jaguar)

Kookaburra

Snake

Spider

CONFUSION, CLEARING UP

Antelope

Black Widow Spider

Blue Whale

Moth

Swan

CONTEMPLATION AND SELF-REFLECTION

Blue Whale

Cat

Chimpanzee

Dragon

Meadowlark

Mole

Mouse

Muskrat

Praying Mantis

Toad

Turtle

Whale

COOPERATION WITH OTHERS

Barred Owl

Bee

Dolphin

Egret

Horse

Jackal

Orca

Pelican

Salamander

Wolf

COURAGE

Bear

Chipmunk

Eagle

Falcon (Peregrine)

Fox (Kit)

Jaguar (Black Jaguar)

Kingfisher

Lion

Mongoose

Musk Ox

Otter

Owl (Screech Owl)

Skunk

Sparrow

Wolverine

CRITICISM AND NEGATIVITY, SHIELDING FROM

Cormorant

Fox (Arctic)

Frog

Goat

Hawk

Hedgehog

Hippopotamus

Horse (White Horse)

Hummingbird

Mongoose

Penguin

Rhinoceros (Black Rhino)

Scorpion

Shark

Tarantula

DEPENDENCIES, BREAKING AWAY FROM UNHEALTHY

Cat (Feral)

Tiger

DEPRESSION, LIFTING

Butterfly

Canary

Cardinal

Coyote

Emu

Hawk

Hummingbird

Robin

DETACHMENT

Eagle

Egret

Gecko

Gila Monster

Heron

Koala

Lizard

Musk Ox

Ram

Salamander

Salmon

Snake

Wombat

DETOXIFICATION, PHYSICAL OR EMOTIONAL

Chinchilla

Cobra

Condor

DEVOTIONAL PRACTICES

Ladybug

DIRECTION WITH YOUR LIFE

Giraffe

Salmon

Starfish

Wolf

Road Runner

Shark

Wolf

DISCERNING TRUTH FROM DECEPTION OR FALSEHOOD

Aardvark

Armadillo

Blue Jay

Bobcat

Chipmunk

Crow

Dragonfly

Fox

Great Horned Owl

Hare

Hippopotamus

Hyena

Lynx

Muskrat

Opossum

Owl

Peacock

Raccoon

Wolf

Wolverine

DREAMING, LUCID

Beluga Whale

Grebe

Groundhog

Jackal

Loon

Penguin

Rattlesnake

EMOTIONAL CLEANSING AND CLEARING

Frog

Pelican

Seal

Toad

Whale (Blue Whale)

EMOTIONAL STRENGTH

Lion

Musk Ox

Polar Bear

Sandpiper

Sea Horse

Seal

Wolverine

EMOTIONS, FEELING AND EXPRESSING

Chameleon

Crane

Duck

Egret

Grebe

Humpback Whale

Orangutan

Polar Bear

Seal

Squirrel

Toucan

Turtle

Whale

Wolf

EMPATHY

Cheetah

Chimpanzee

Dolphin

Gorilla

Grebe

Horse

Koala

Starfish

ENDURING DIFFICULT TIMES

Camel

Eagle

Gazelle

Lizard

Llama

Moose

Musk Ox

Penguin

Pheasant

EXPRESSING YOURSELF CLEARLY AND CONCISELY

Chimpanzee

Dolphin

Gorilla

Kingfisher

Orangutan

Sparrow

Squirrel

Wolf

FAITH, INCREASING OR KEEPING YOUR

Camel

Dog

Giraffe

Kinkajou

Ladybug

Polar Bear

Puffin

Stag

Swan

Wolverine

FEAR, OVERCOMING AND RELEASING

Gorilla

Great Horned Owl

Jaguar (Black Jaguar)

Kingfisher

Kiwi

Ladybug

Pelican

Polar Bear

Snake

Spider

Whale

FORGIVENESS

Coyote

Pelican

Penguin

FRIENDLINESS

Dolphin

Giraffe

GENTLENESS
Deer
Rhinoceros
Stag

GETTING UNSTUCK
Black Widow Spider
Emu
Heron
Horse
Jellyfish
Kangaroo
Salamander
Seal
Sloth
Spider
Squirrel
Wasp
Weasel
Zebra

GIVING TO OTHERS
Duck
Gnu
Kiwi
Manatee
Pelican
Quail
Sandpiper
Scorpion
Sparrow
Starfish

Turkey

GRATITUDE, FOCUS ON
Crane
Quail
Swan

GROUNDED AND CENTERED, GETTING OR STAYING
Baboon
Cheetah
Dove
Emu
Gorilla
Hippopotamus
Kiwi
Meerkat
Mole
Ostrich
Pheasant
Praying Mantis
Salamander
Sandpiper
Seal
Tortoise
Wasp

HAPPINESS, SEEKING
Hummingbird
Lark
Robin
Unicorn

HEALING, EMOTIONAL

Bear
Cow
Crow
Flamingo
Macaw
Osprey
Otter
Parrot
Platypus
Rattlesnake
Raven
Snake
Tiger

HEALING RELATIONSHIPS

Cow
Rattlesnake

HUMOR, KEEPING OR REGAINING A SENSE OF

Coyote
Dingo
Duck (Wood Duck)
Hyena
Kookaburra
Puffin

INNER WISDOM, ACCESSING YOUR

Heron (Great Blue Heron)
Ibis
Lark

Owl
Peacock
Praying Mantis
Rabbit
Rhinoceros
Salmon
Snake
Spider
Tortoise
Turtle
Wolf

INSIGHT AND UNDERSTANDING

Ferret
Hawk
Kinkajou
Leopard
Macaw
Platypus
Whale
Wolf
Woodpecker

INSPIRATION AND POSITIVE SUPPORT

Deer
Eagle (Bald Eagle)
Goose
Monkey
Orca
Parrot
Penguin
Rabbit

Salamander

Sparrow

Swallow

Walrus

Whale

INTENTION, CLEAR AND PURPOSEFUL

Cougar

Falcon

Great Horned Owl

Grouse (Ruffed Grouse)

Jaguar

Lynx

Magpie

Penguin

Raven

Robin

Salmon

Shark

Sparrow

Squirrel

Stag

Wombat

JOY

Hummingbird

Robin

Sea Lion

Sparrow

Whale

JUDGMENTS AND ASSESSMENTS OF OTHERS OR SITUATION

Antelope

Ferret

Lizard

Opossum

LISTENING SKILLS

Dolphin

Giraffe

Gorilla

Lynx

Magpie

Sea Lion

Seagull

Tortoise

Turtle

LOVE, EXPRESSING

Butterfly

Cockatoo

Dog

Dove

Hummingbird

Kiwi

Penguin

Rabbit

Snow Leopard

Sparrow

Swallow

Wolf

MIRACLES, HAVING FAITH IN

Beluga Whale

Horse (White Horse)

Rhinoceros (White Rhino)

Unicorn

White Buffalo

NATURAL RHYTHMS AND CYCLES, ATTUNING TO

Falcon

Gila Monster

Goat

Grouse

Jellyfish

Kinkajou

Seal

Swan

Woodpecker

NATURE AND THE EARTH, CONNECTING WITH

Blackbird

Cassowary

Gibbon

Goat

Gorilla

Hummingbird

Kiwi

Meadowlark

Praying Mantis

Seagull

Wolverine

Woodpecker

OPTIMISM

Giraffe

Hedgehog

Hummingbird

Pheasant

Rabbit

OVERCOMING EMOTIONAL OBSTACLES AND ENTANGLEMENTS

Duck

Elephant

Goat

Hawk

Horse

Leopard

Meadowlark

Pelican

Snow Leopard

PATIENCE WITH OTHERS

Horse

Mongoose

Penguin

PEACE AND HARMONY

White Buffalo

Dove

Jellyfish

Kingfisher

Puffin

Rhinoceros

Whale

POWER, CLAIMING AND OWNING YOUR

Cormorant

Cougar

Grouse

Horse

Jaguar

Komodo Dragon

Polar Bear

Python

Rattlesnake

Raven

Scorpion

Stag

Tiger

PRAYER

Eagle

Koala

Ladybug

Praying Mantis

Puffin

Raven

Scorpion

PRESENCE, STRONG

Eagle

Cougar

Goshawk

Hedgehog

Hummingbird

Jaguar

Komodo Dragon

Lion

Mockingbird

Parrot

Polar Bear

Raven

Wolf

PROTECTION, EMOTIONAL OR PSYCHIC

Armadillo

Crab

Echidna

Goose

Hawk

Horse (White Horse)

Hummingbird

Ladybug

Lynx

Mockingbird

Penguin

Porcupine

Rhinoceros

Seal

Shark

Swallow

Turtle

Whale

Wolf

PROTECTION FROM ALL HARM

Bear

Dog

Dragon

Gorilla

Jackal

Leopard

Polar Bear

Rhinoceros (Black Rhino)

Shark

Weasel

Wolf

Woodpecker

REBIRTH AND RENEWAL

Bat

Butterfly

Kite

Leopard

Python

Rattlesnake

Raven

Robin

Salmon

Snake

Stag

Stork

RECONCILING YOUR PAST

Lemur

Lizard

Penguin

Pigeon

Rattlesnake

Raven

Swallow

Toad

RELATIONSHIP HARMONY

Dove

Goose

Jackal

Meadowlark

RELEASING AND CLEARING WHAT NO LONGER FITS

Frog

Hummingbird

Jaguar

Kookaburra

Leopard

Lobster

Mongoose

Mouse

Ostrich

Pelican

Praying Mantis

Python

Rat

Rattlesnake

Robin

Snake

Sparrow

Squirrel

Stag

Tarantula

Toad

Wolf

Turkey

Turtle

Whale

Woodpecker

RELEASING GUILT AND SHAME

Hummingbird

Pelican

Penguin

Rattlesnake

Snake

RELEASING NEGATIVITY AND JUDGMENTS

Cuckoo

Deer

Emu

Frog

Hummingbird

Pelican

Rattlesnake

Snake

RELEASING TOXICITIES

Condor (Turkey Vulture)

Rattlesnake

Scorpion

Snake

Spider (Brown Spider)

RESPECT AND CARE FOR THE EARTH

Jaguar

RESPECT FOR OTHERS

Gorilla

Great Horned Owl

Kite

Porcupine

Skunk

Starfish

Wombat

SACRED OR PERSONAL SPACE, ESTABLISHING

Cassowary

Grouse (Sage Grouse)

Kingfisher

Koala

Panda

Rhinoceros

Tiger

SOUL'S PATH, STAYING TRUE TO YOUR

Deer

Dolphin

Hippopotamus

Salmon

Wolf

SOUL'S PURPOSE AND MISSION, CLARITY ABOUT YOUR

Cassowary

Dolphin

Gnu

Mockingbird

Quail

Salmon

Wolf

Zebra

SPIRITUAL AWARENESS AND GROWTH

White Buffalo

Dolphin

Dove

Duck (Wood Duck)

Emu

Gazelle

Giraffe

Goose

Goshawk

Hippopotamus

Horse

Macaw

Moose

Ostrich

Owl

Raven

Robin

Sandpiper

Snake

Whale

STORYTELLING

Lark

Whale

Wolf

STRESS MANAGEMENT

Dolphin

Elk

Gila Monster

Koala

Leopard

Manatee

Opossum

Tortoise

Turtle

TRANSFORMATION

Butterfly

Eel

Ibis

Lobster

Python

Rattlesnake

Salamander

Salmon

Scorpion

Snake

Toad

TRUSTING YOUR PERCEPTIONS

Macaw

Otter

Salmon

Weasel

TRUSTING YOUR SENSES

Armadillo

Chameleon

Elephant

Fox

Goat

Moose

Moth

Muskrat

Salmon

Seagull

Snake

Squirrel

Tarantula

Weasel

TRUST IN DIVINE ORDER AND TIMING

Cuckoo

Otter

Pheasant

Robin

Stag

VEGETARIAN DIET

Elk

Kinkajou

Koala

Porcupine

Prairie Dog

Rabbit

Tortoise

VICTIM, RELEASING BELIEF THAT YOU'RE A

Condor

Cormorant

Dingo

Pelican

Robin

Sparrow

WORRY, LETTING GO OF

Boar

Bull

Crane

Otter

Peacock

Red Panda

Turtle

Unicorn

MEET OUR SACRED STORYTELLERS

SZILVIA BARTHA is a leather crafter, archer, táltos drummer, Warrior Woman Training camp co-founder, Hungarian cultural preservationist, and guardian of ancient Magyar traditions in America. She lives in sunny California.

DR. DAN BEAUPRE, a dentist, and **SARA BEAUPRE,** a registered dental hygienist, reside in Reedsville, Wisconsin with their bird dogs Zuri and River.

FLORENTINE BISSCHOPS is a licensed spiritual-intuitive mentor and healer, animal communicator, and shamanic practitioner. She assists her international clients (animals and humans alike) in shifting and healing their emotional wounds.

HELEN BRENNAND is an equine professional, holistic therapist, and author. The Haven in England is home to Helen and The Herd. Together, they connect beyond physical reality to unearth the deep magical wisdom of the horse.

LISA MARIE BYARS is a poet and dreamer, certified ERYT yoga teacher, and reiki master who also teaches autistic students. She finds her happy place in Santa Cruz, California.

ANNE CEDERBERG is a professional naturalist, artist, and writer. Her mission is to help others see the God in nature. She lives in Florida.

CHRIS CIEPIELA has the desire to convey the magic in the mundane through healing arts and writing. She lives in western Massachusetts with her spouse, Lindsay, two boys, Luca and Mateo, and their dog, Georgia.

STACY CORLEY ≈ **A.P.** is a spiritual entrepreneur, nurse by day, and spiritual always, living breath to breath. Her awakening began in 1996 and her toolbox is full of goodies. alternatepossibili2.wixsite.com/altposs.

KATHLEEN CROW is a retired second-grade teacher who believes in miracles, and loves books and lazy days. She lives in Montana with her husband, Aussiedoodle puppy, and three-legged cat.

GINA DRELLACK is a writer, teacher, reiki master, and author of *This Time, Glide: Stop Struggling for Success and Begin Achieving through Ease and Joy.* ginadrellack. com.

JOHN PAUL (EAGLE HEART) FISCHBACH is a theatre and film director, an initiated shaman, and a sacred pipe carrier and site whisperer. He is the host and creator of the international documentary series, *The Shaman and the Stones.*

ROBERT V. GERARD is an internationally published author and holistic psychologist who specializes in human-spiritual philosophy. His book, *Welcome to Spirituality*, is due to be released soon. oughten-house.com.

LAURA E. GÓMEZ is a therapist who guides others to listen to and trust their inner wisdom. She was born on the beautiful island of Puerto Rico and grew up in the small beach town, Luquillo, where she felt an innate connection to nature and animals and learned to trust their guidance.

DR. JOANNE HALVERSON is a psychotherapist, professor, spiritual mentor, and healer, and author of several research articles in the field of psychology. She lived off grid for many years and studied with native shamans from the matriarchal Northwest Coast Salish tribes.

ADAIR WILSON HEITMANN is an award-winning artist. Her writing is featured in three anthologies, and in articles about creativity, wellness, nature, writing, and the mind/body/spirit connection.

LISA M. JONES is an empath, intuitive, artist, teacher, photographer, and ER/mental health R.N. who is certified as an Angel Alchemist, and in ThetaHealing and Seraphin Blueprint. She has a B.S.N. in nursing and M.F.A. in studio arts. Lisa has witnessed healing for people and animals with the Divine, angels, and spirit guides. soulfullmessenger.com.

TAMARA KNOX, M.MSC, PH.D., PSYTHD. is an international bestselling author and Theocentric Psychology enthusiast. She uses breath, sound, movement, consciousness, and food energetics to explore metaphysical and multidimensional realms. shekhinahpath.com.

JUDY LEMON is a shamanic practitioner and certified trauma therapist with a private practice in Southern California. She is currently caretaker to Sirena, a medicine cat, and a yard full of crows. judylemon.com.

EILEEN LOVE has found the beauty and restorative power of nature to be her faithful constant in an occasionally turbulent life. "Nature fills me up, poetry fills me up, writing fills me up," she says, "and always noticing love and beauty where some might think they are not."

EMILY MCCAY is a short-fiction author whose 15-year, inner-work practice has incorporated the Enneagram, integrative breathwork, and ecstatic/shamanic journeying.

DR. THOMAS C. MCGARRITY has spent four years exploring experiential mysticism through his doctoral research and dissertation. His story in this book comes directly from his work.

MISA MYERS has an extensive background in education, a commitment to social justice, and is a writer. With amazing children and an incredible "ride-or-die" life partner, Misa considers herself to be one lucky woman.

KATE NELIGAN is a bestselling author, TEDx speaker, animal communicator/healer, and equine-partnered life/business coach who pairs spiritual psychology tools with the intuitive healing power of horses. kateneligan.com.

NANCY PROULX is a lifelong equestrian who is helping to expand the healing potential of working with horses. Her coaching practice and horse wisdom programs help individuals explore personal empowerment and intuitive development.

REV. STEPHANIE RED FEATHER, PH.D. is a divine feminine change agent, the award-winning, bestselling author of *The Evolutionary Empath: A Practical Guide for Heart-Centered Consciousness*, Empath Activation Cards, and contributing author of two other books. bluestartemple.org.

SAMANTHA ROE is an animal reiki teacher and practitioner, animal communicator, and an oracle and angel card reader. She is on a mission to help animals and people heal, thereby providing empowerment to all.

LAURA S. ROWLEY is the host of *Animal Connections with Laura Rowley* on Dreamvisions7RadioNetwork, broadcast in more than 106 countries, and a contributor to *Mayhem to Miracles: Sacred Stories of Transformational Hope*. Laura's unique perspective of the world is one in which animals not only have a voice, but also wisdom to impart to their human companions.

MIA RUSINKO is a psychic medium, intuitive life coach, spiritual teacher, and motivational speaker. Mia found her passion and purpose after a near-death experience shifted her perspective on life and death.

KATHA SAGER is a medium, teacher, and author with a passion for helping others. Spirit guided Katha to start her business, Sager's Sacred Space, and to publish the Sacred Bird Oracle, in order to help others.

KAREN B. SHEA is an author, photographer, and nature lover. Her desire to teach children about the natural world led to publishing her book, *Clark the Mountain Beaver and His Big Adventure!* A passionate advocate for the environment, she continues to use her skills to inspire others about this amazing world. clarkthemountainbeaver.com.

BERNIE SIEGEL, M.D. is a leading teacher of the mind-body connection and well known for his *New York Times* bestselling book *Love, Medicine and Miracles*. Bernie is also the author of the novel *Three Men, Six Lives* and co-author with his grandson, Charlie Siegel, of *When You Realize How Perfect Everything Is*, a book of short writings and poetry.

TELA TALISE is a professor, artist, and writer from New Jersey. As the founder of My Path Inspired, she creates symbolic, nature-based art and blogs about nature inspired living. mypathinspired.com.

YOLANDA TONG is a Melbourne, Australia-based direct voice channeler who supports intuitives, healers, and wellness practitioners in developing their unique gifts and growing into their potential.

SARYON MICHAEL WHITE is an author and channel for Spirit. His first book, *Roya Sands and the Bridge Between Worlds*, is a highly relevant spiritual adventure set in the modern world. saryon.com.

MEET OUR FEATURED AUTHOR

DR. STEVEN FARMER is a licensed psychotherapist, shamanic practitioner, and author of several best-selling books and oracle cards, including *Animal Spirit Guides, Pocket Guide to Spirit Animals, Sacred Ceremony, Healing Ancestral Karma, Earth Magic, Earth Magic Oracle Cards,* and *Children's Spirit Animal Cards.*

Dr. Farmer offers individual consultations in person or remotely by Zoom. He draws from a wealth of training and experience as a psychotherapist, shamanic healer, and trauma recovery specialist. Dr. Farmer offers a popular private mentoring program and serves on the board of the Society of Shamanic Practice.

Learn more at drstevenfarmer.com.